'The story gives an inside p
and also how those outside o
make a difference. The stor
has questions about the
someone in it.'
Paul Sydnor, Europe Regional Leader, IAFR, RHP Network Leader

'What makes this book special in my eyes is that Javed, Nasreen, Nimra and Aroon kept looking for hope in whatever situation they were in, regardless of how they felt. They tried to look at every situation with God's eyes. They were always looking for God's guidance and for opportunities to build bridges, to use their talents and to give love to the people they met.'
Diana Baan, Fieldworker, Stichting Gave

'This book clearly shows on which points the COA, the IND and the Repatriation & Departure Service could humanise their working methods with a few simple measures, because despite the many good things they do, very poignant aspects are revealed, of which I am deeply ashamed as a Dutchman! I heartily recommend this book to you to gain some insight into the circumstances that so many refugees face daily.'
Hans van Delft, Chairman IWAK in Katwijk aan Zee

'The Bible says in 2 Timothy 3:12 that "everyone who wants to live a godly life in Christ Jesus will be persecuted". We see this once again proven in the life of Javed and his family. What a testimony they provide in the way they persevered through the asylum procedure.'
Maarten Dees, President of Open Doors International, Netherlands

'Once a family arrives in the Netherlands to seek asylum, there is still a long road ahead. The experiences in this book give us a glimpse into all the emotions and practical issues that refugees have to deal with every day. From the smallest things that we all take for granted, like finding a Wi-Fi spot, to the daily challenges of finding Bed, Bath and Bread.'
Fr Sjaak de Boer, Mill Hill, Pastor of the RC Church of Our Saviour

'This book ... is not only engaging, but also powerful and very personal. I work with refugees in Italy and understand first-hand some of the trials these folks face on a daily basis. For all who are called to serve and share the gospel with refugees, this book is a must-read, and gives a rare and profound inside perspective of the refugee world in Europe.'
Leonard Xerri, Missionary, Avant Ministries

'A "must-read" for anyone who is genuinely involved with refugees, who wants to understand them and wants to stand by them. I hope that many people will read this book. In particular, I hope that church congregations will take the content of this book to heart in order to understand their calling to "the stranger at our gate". Highly recommended!'
Rev C H Hogendoorn, Reformed Church Katwijk aan Zee

'This book is a must for anyone who wants to know more about what it means to be an asylum seeker and the hardships that entails. ... The power of the book is a simple testimony not to be overcome by this, but to see the good in every situation.'
Rev Piet Vroegindeweij, Reformed Church, Lexmond

'How good is it that Javed gives us an insight into the life of a Pakistani Christian who arrives as a refugee in the Netherlands with his family ... Heartily recommended.'
Joël Voordewind, Member of Parlement-ChristenUnie

'Faith and good will help to overcome even the deepest crisis – that is the message that this book gives us all.'
Rev R H M de Jonge, Reformed Church

'An impressive, moving, yet inspiring narration ... At some places their story is painful to read. There are moments of hope, and some of despair. But it is told always with the example of Christ in mind!'

'Javed and his family practised the words of the gospel, even in the darkest moments of their life. "God taught us to trust him", is the key message he gives us.

'An inspiring message, from a family that was supported by the pillars of their faith.'
Marten van der Meer, Parochiekern Joannes de Doper, Katwijk

'It is a book that not only tells the life story of a family, but it will also help believers and churches in their interactions with refugees. I hope and wish that it will be a blessing to many.'
Marianne, Javed's mentor in the integration project of (the municipality of) Leiden

'The honesty of this book really struck me ... This book also shows how loving one's neighbour and praising God can be practised in both the smaller and the bigger things, which is a great word of encouragement for every Christian to incorporate into their daily life.'
Mirjam, Dutch Christian student, Leiden

'This book is a fascinating, beautiful and moving report of their journey. The refugee in our midst lives so close and yet in a different world.'
Fr Michel Hagen, Parish Priest, H. Augustinus (Katwijk)

'In Javed's story, we see an inspiring example of steadfast faith in a God who can be trusted. Time and time again, facing challenging circumstances, Javed put his trust in the promises in God's word, and with prayer and thanksgiving made his needs known to his heavenly Father.'
Revd Ruan Crew, Chaplain, St James Voorschoten; Area Dean of the Netherlands, Diocese in Europe

'This story illustrates, among other things, how learning Dutch has helped Javed and his family to become familiar with the Dutch culture as well as to establish relationships with the people living in this country.'
Marjolein van der Plas, English Language Teacher

'The Dutch Catholic priest, Henri Nouwen, once said, "Ministry is entering with our human brokenness into communion with others and speaking a word of hope." The refugee experience shared by Javed's family is that resounding voice of hope and living faith.'
Mark Farrell, Catechist at RC Church of Our Saviour, The Hague

No Longer Strangers?

Javed Masih

instant
apostle

First published in Great Britain in 2019

Instant Apostle
The Barn
1 Watford House Lane
Watford
Herts
WD17 1BJ

British Library Cataloguing-in-Publication Data

A catalogue record for this book is available from the British Library

This book and all other Instant Apostle books are available from Instant Apostle:

Website: www.instantapostle.com

E-mail: info@instantapostle.com

ISBN 978-1-912726-03-5

Printed in Great Britain

Contents

Foreword

This is a book about the strength of God.

At the same time, it is also a story of an ordinary man, Javed Masih, and his family. By listening to God and not giving up, he makes a difference where God has placed him. In Pakistan, Javed learned to fully follow his God in times of affliction. In Western Europe, he continues to live this way and is an example for Christians here.

A few months after our first meeting in 2016, Javed and I sat in my office. He told me what his life in Pakistan was like: Christians (approximately 1.6 per cent of the population) had difficulty in this Islamic country. This hurt him. He recounted how Christians were pushed into the margins of society. The influential jobs were not for them, and their development was lagging behind.

Javed organised an after-school tutoring programme for children from poor Christian families, so that they would be given better opportunities in society. The tutoring programme became more and more widespread until, at last, hundreds of children were receiving additional education. Javed had to act cautiously. Extremist groups were becoming more active and more radical in Pakistan. Their crimes were hardly punished by the government. It was dangerous to stand out as a Christian.

That Javed does not avoid pain and confrontation was also apparent when he heard in 2013 of the horrible attack on a church in Peshawar. Extremists exploded two bombs, 169 people died and 130 were wounded. Javed travelled there immediately and arrived shortly after the attack. He helped to take care of the wounded and was at the burial of the dead. He walked along in the protests that followed against the lack of security for Christians and against radical groups that deem themselves untouchable.

Javed wrote a book about a Christian Pakistani parliamentarian who stood up for religious minorities and was killed. After the book was published, it did not sit well with the fanatical groups. As a result, Javed and his family had to flee from Pakistan.

'How did you do all that?' I asked him. 'How did you know you had to do this?'

'If there are difficult things, I always think what God would have done. And that I'm going to do,' said Javed.

The simplicity of his faith and his trust in God moved me. The risks were not important. Neither was the wait for a special epiphany, such as a voice from heaven. *Just do what God would do.* As David did when he approached Goliath without a special commission from God, but driven by the injustice he observed. Being fully prepared to be God's hands and feet on earth. Wanting to be the body of Christ. The body of Christ, prepared to suffer when needed.

The start in the Netherlands was difficult for the family. This book concerns their first years in the Netherlands. The lengthy asylum procedure, the uncertainty and the emptiness almost became too much for Javed. Yet his strength of mind was not broken. He managed to fall back on the question that also directed his actions in Pakistan: 'What would God have done now?' By allowing God to determine their course, Javed and his wife, Nasreen, together with their children, Aroon and Nimra, found the courage to continue in depressing circumstances.

This is a story of a man who left his country, because of a situation of great affliction, and had to flee to Western Europe. It tells us how we can be moved by sadness and injustice; how to listen to the Spirit of God. Javed's story shows us how to stand where God has placed us. It is no tale of great wonders. It is rather a tale of obedience and endurance. It is a route open for every Christian who wants to follow God obediently.

Romans 5:3-4 says: 'Not only so, but we also glory in our sufferings, because we know that suffering produces perseverance; perseverance, character; and character, hope.'

Jan Pieter Mostert, Director, Stichting Gave

About Javed Masih and Family

Javed Masih is from Pakistan. He grew up as part of the Christian minority in Pakistan, since the country is predominantly Muslim. After his father died, when Javed was nine, he and his two sisters were raised by their mother. Although the family was poor, they held the strong belief that education brings change in people's lives. Through his family's hard work, Javed was able to attend a school ten kilometres away from his village and stay at a boarding house during the school terms. Whenever there was a break from school, he contributed to his tuition by working in the fields, like his mother. Javed's mother died when he was sixteen. But she had given him a clear vision, a foundation of education, and a heart for service to others.

Javed earned a bachelor's degree in Religious Education and Pastoral Studies from the National Catechists' Training Centre in Khushpur, Faisalabad. Then, he began a career of pastoral and social work in Pakistan that was focused largely around the following scripture from the Gospel of Matthew:

> For I was hungry and you gave me food, I was thirsty and you gave me something to drink, I was a stranger and you welcomed me, I was naked and you gave me clothing, I was sick and you took care of me, I was in prison and you visited me.
>
> *Matthew 25:35-36 (NRSV)*

Despite having so many economic constraints, Javed never looked back; he earned Bachelor's degrees in both arts and education. After that he managed to secure three Master's degrees in Urdu literature, human resource management, and theology in peace, trauma and religion. In addition, he undertook some courses in Italian language and literature, research work, capacity building training, trauma and facilitator in dialogue for peaceful change.

In April of 1997, Javed married Nasreen and gained a partner in his vocation and his mission. They had their daughter, Nimra, in 1998 and their son, Aroon, in 1999.

In February of 1999, Javed founded a school for poor children in Rawalpindi. His motivation for beginning the school came from the idea that neglected and marginalised people have the power to improve their lives only through education. The people Javed wanted to help were living in conditions below the poverty line. At the start, the community was being served by a priest, who visited and said Holy Mass once a month. Javed needed a space to hold classes, so he volunteered to lead Bible services on the other Sundays in exchange for the use of the service room for his school. In this humble space, St Peter's school was born.

Over time, with much work and through God's providence, both the school and the church community grew. The school was able to purchase land and construct its own building. Likewise, the church became large enough to have a chapel, named St Stephen's. Javed wrote his first book for this new church: a liturgy book of worship and prayer. Javed chose to leave his position as manager of St Peter's school in 2006, to allow the community to assume responsibility. Today, the school functions as a middle school. Javed sees St Peter's school as a concrete illustration of how God is able to create things where once there was nothing.

Javed worked with youth for a year as a coordinator at Interfaith Harmony, where he worked to increase understanding and peace between people of different religions. The initiative brought social and interfaith harmony at a grass-roots level. Then, he worked as an Italian language teacher for some years in Islamabad. Throughout this time, Nasreen was working as a high school teacher at the parish school in Rawalpindi. The couple would spend the first part of their days at their jobs, and the second part of their days conducting social and pastoral work as volunteers. Some of the pastoral work was in other cities, while other work was in the local diocese where Javed was a catechist.[1] Javed and Nasreen conducted gospel-sharing meetings for the community, so the people could receive Christian formation and learn how to live the gospel values with integrity.

---

[1] Someone who teaches Catholic catechism in parishes in the Catholic Church in Pakistan, but as a layperson.

As part of their volunteer work, Javed and Nasreen worked in disaster management for refugees and internally displaced persons. They did works of mercy by conducting local collections of food, clothing and other basic necessities. Then, they brought the collected items to people in the camps. The focus of this work was more than just providing material goods. Javed and Nasreen felt their true help was given in listening to people's stories, offering support and providing love. They strove to create a spirit of unity, fraternity and friendship with the peple.

Javed continued to support education as a tool for change in his volunteer work. From 2011 to 2013, he created an after-school tutoring programme for poor children in Rawalpindi. In Pakistan, the first diploma is given in Grade 10. To receive this diploma, students must pass tests in compulsory subjects. In general, students were weak in English and mathematics. Javed worked with local schools and teachers to create a programme that would give students extra help in these subjects for the six months leading up to the important diploma exams. Nearly 1,100 students received after-school coaching, from fifty teachers, as a result of the programme. The coaching classes allowed students who could not afford extra tutoring the opportunity to improve their performance in exams.

In the midst of this professional and volunteer work, Javed wrote a second book, which was published in 2014. This book was about a Pakistani Christian parliamentarian for Religious Minority Affairs who was assassinated by fanatical groups. After the book was published, it did not sit well with the fanatical groups. As a result, Javed and his family had to flee from Pakistan. This is how Javed, Nasreen and their two teenage children came to the Netherlands in August 2014.

You may ask yourself why Javed and his family took the step of writing this book about their experiences as refugees. This book answers questions, including: what is it like to be a refugee? How do refugees see the challenges, needs and demands? What is their vision of hopes and struggles for the future in this place? And, how do they rely on God in their day-to-day life?

As a family, they thought it would be very important for society, the Church and other development organisations to know what the real situation is in asylum centres and how the people there embrace difficulties.

During their stay in the asylum centre, they found that so many volunteers, social workers and church groups were involved in different ways to help the refugees; but sometimes they did not exactly know what to do for them in this uncertain situation.

Thank you for your interest in reading this book. Hopefully, as you read Javed's story, you will gain some information about daily life in asylum centres that helps you to grow in your own involvement, ministry and compassion towards the people who live there.

Lastly, Javed and his family are forever indebted to everyone who offered their encouragement, friendship and interest in bringing their story to book form. They are of course indebted to all the people who supplied their comments. They are grateful as well to the publisher and his professional team who published the book.

Note: This book is written from Javed's point of view, but it is really a family story. Each family member has contributed to completing this book.

You can continue to follow Javed and his family at
https://www.facebook.com/BookNoLongerStrangers

Introduction

Imagine leaving the place where you were born, had grown up, gone to school, met your spouse and started your family; saying farewell to family and friends, and realising that the separation may be a permanent one; leaving your profession, your church and your community behind, and beginning a new life in a foreign environment. This is what an asylum seeker does when they leave their home in order to keep themselves and their loved ones safe – they become a stranger. This is what Javed Masih and his family did when they left Pakistan and were resettled in the Netherlands. This book is their story, an account of their experiences in a time of great uncertainty.

When Javed, his wife, Nasreen, and their two teenage children arrived in a refugee camp in the Netherlands, their first set of challenges were in adjusting to the seemingly endless new experiences: different language, culture, food, clothing and weather. The title of 'stranger' also brought change. The family felt the weight of their homelessness, loneliness, isolation and uncertainty.

In the midst of such turmoil, Javed and his family turned to the Lord for strength and inspiration. Slowly, with constant prayer and hard work, they began to develop harmony and solidarity with others in the camp. They found that, even though the life of someone in a refugee camp may seem insignificant, the presence of God can be revealed in all circumstances. In addition to building a community within their camp, Javed and his family also began interacting with the Dutch community. They started visiting the local library to learn to speak Dutch, and found a church to attend.

After three months in camp, the family was transferred and began a long legal process of seeking asylum in the Netherlands. Much of that time was spent at the camp in Katwijk, where Javed and his family shared an apartment with others. The four of them slept in one room and shared a bathroom and toilet with the occupants of the other bedroom. Thirteen apartments shared a communal kitchen and a laundry room. This is where Javed lived for nearly twenty months. The time there was filled with uncertainty and instability, because the asylum process was slow. The family was waiting for a final decision, to hear if they would be granted permission to remain in the Netherlands.

During that period, there were dark times, depression, and instances when Javed's hope and faith were tested. There were also times of delight, when humanity's diversity came together in harmony to create wonderful memories. The difficult period ended with the joyful news that the family had been granted permission to reside in the Netherlands. However, Javed and his family realised that God was present in both the darkness and the light.

While you may never experience what Javed did, every person faces uncertainty in their life. No one knows what the future will hold. As you read Javed's story, I invite you to use what he learned during the turmoil of uncertainty to reflect upon your own circumstances. There is hope in the gospel. Leaving a position of comfort and moving towards an unknown destination – whatever the conditions – can be difficult and uncomfortable. However, if we leave ourselves in God's hands, He will always amaze us with His provision.

Courtney Knott, Catechism Teacher, Religious Education – Church of Our Saviour, Den Haag

Chapter One
Unknown Destination

Every person has those moments in their life that are unforgettable. Some moments are good and some are bad. These moments become a part of our memories. No matter how hard we try, we can't get them out of our mind. We also have those dark moments that change our lives forever. In those moments our whole world is turned upside down and we feel like everything has stopped.

We strongly believe that circumstances end but memories last forever. Here we recall some of those moments, which occurred at the time when we had to flee from our country because of certain circumstances and travel to the Netherlands.

When our plane arrived in Dubai, it was early morning, usually the time when our children left for school and we left for our work. But on that day we had to leave everything behind. Our children were thinking about their schools, books, uniforms, classmates and teachers, while my wife and I were thinking about our work, workplaces and colleagues – and we were feeling grief in our hearts. We shared all these emotions with each other.

While we were waiting for our next flight, to Amsterdam, we sat in the waiting room where many Dutch people were sitting and talking to each other. At that particular time, we wondered how we were going to survive in the Netherlands. We couldn't understand a single word that they were saying.

At that time, we didn't know that the Dutch could speak English. When there was an announcement about our flight, we all looked anxiously at each other and then went and sat in the plane. That journey felt like we were walking on thorns. Everything was very painful.

As the plane was approaching the Netherlands, our uncertainties increased. What kind of challenges would we have to face? What did our future hold?

These were unanswered questions full of doubts. Although we knew that we were going to the Netherlands, we still didn't know what our final destination would be. We had no feelings of stability or firmness. Everything was uncertain, fearful and unstable.

When we landed in the Netherlands, we were terrified. We felt like all eyes were on us at the airport. The whole family felt unbalanced. It was one of the darkest periods in our lives.

So many times we felt useless, worthless and unsuccessful in this painful situation, but gradually we entered into the feeling of placing our trust in God, even in an unknown destination. We tried to learn to trust God with an open heart in times of uncertainty and doubt.

We have also learned that God intervenes in our lives; God comes to us through known and unknown people, events, happenings, experiences and places. God became a human being in the person of His Son, Jesus Christ, sharing our sufferings, our life and our day-to-day problems.

The journey towards an unknown destination is a journey of life, a journey of faith. It is an experience of intimacy and living in God deeply, to come to Jesus and to remain with Him. As 1 John 4:13 states, 'This is how we know that we live in him and he in us: he has given us of his Spirit.'

Finally, we left Schiphol airport and departed to an unknown destination, remembering the words of Jesus: 'Do not let your hearts be troubled. You believe in God; believe also in me. My Father's house has many rooms' (John 14:1-2). We also remembered His words in John 14:18: 'I will not leave you as orphans; I will come to you.'

Chapter Two
Challenges and Faith

We arrived at Ter Apel on 11th August 2014. After the initial interviews, we were sent into the refugee camp for two days with some instructions, regulations, a programme and an agenda. We were handed some packets of basic needs before we went into the living area. When we entered our room, there were already two families sleeping where we, too, were supposed to live. Now, including ourselves, we were thirteen people living there. There were communal toilets and bathrooms in the living area. Sometimes, someone forgot to flush the toilet or did not use the bathroom properly.

Our first impression of the room was that it was very untidy and strange. This was the very first experience in our lives, as a family, of having to live with strangers. Everything was varied, including language, ethnicity, tradition, norms, background, food, dress and ages. Therefore, we could not immediately develop relationships with one another.

We all were unknown to each other, all our languages were different and we could not speak one shared language between us . We had different cultures, customs, social and religious contexts, and backgrounds. Therefore, we were often a complete mystery to one another, even though we tried to reveal ourselves to each other. At that moment, there was only one thing which was the source of our happiness and motivation: the protection of our lives. Hence, we were feeling secure and safe.

At this place, we used to go for breakfast, lunch and dinner in the dining hall, where we would see more than 500 people from different countries. We always waited in the queue to get food. It was totally different food from what we were used to. It was difficult to eat something so foreign to our taste, but we accepted it as a challenge.

The weather was also becoming more of a challenge each day. Unexpectedly, the heavy rain began, causing the temperature to change from warm to cold. All of us who were living there without appropriate clothing were provided with some warm clothes.

From that moment, we started to understand what it meant to be refugees. Although we had read in the newspapers and seen the movies about the life of refugees, in real life the experience was totally different. We found ourselves living in an atmosphere where everybody seemed sad and depressed. It could easily be seen on others' faces – the challenges, questions, and disappointment that they were feeling yet, at the same time, some hope at the thought of seeking (and being granted) asylum.

All our challenges appeared in the form of things we had not experienced before: a different language, culture, customs, communications, food, dress, hygiene and weather, as well as homelessness, migration, loneliness, isolation and lack of social relationships. At that moment, as we were facing all of these challenges, we remembered the Holy Family (Joseph, Mary and their child, Jesus) when they became refugees in Egypt. We thought of their experience of migration and of being refugees. As a result, we tried to see our challenges as a process of growing in our faith, a process of hope, of discovering the love of God, and of gaining a better understanding of ourselves and others.

In the evenings, we had prayer times and said the Holy Rosary together. We began to present our problems and challenges before God with strong faith. We do believe that God reveals Himself in life's realities, in events, in challenges and in everyday happenings. He also reveals Himself among common, simple and ordinary people.

In spite of all of those challenges, there was one thing that was very positive and remarkable, which inspired us. All of us who arrived there as refugees, and made an application for asylum, came with different fears, difficulties, traumas and agonies. However, all of us were heartily welcomed by the staff and management at Ter Apel. The management at this centre was very kind, polite, professional, caring, cooperative and generous.

With mixed feelings of happiness and sorrow, we left Ter Apel and were transferred to Budel for three months.

Chapter Three
Be Practical

It was the afternoon of 13th August 2014 when we left for Budel. There were almost fifty of us, belonging to different countries. During the journey, there were so many questions going through our minds about the new camp. Would it have the same atmosphere as Ter Apel or would it be different? We arrived there with all of these mixed and uncertain thoughts and feelings.

When we arrived at the camp reception, some of the staff of the Centraal Orgaan opvang asielzoekers (COA)[2] were there to receive us. While we streamed out of the bus, we noticed that the people who were already living there were looking at us intently, obviously hoping to find somebody from their own countries.

The COA took all of us to an information hall, where we were given information, instructions and basic necessary goods such as food, towels, blankets, bed sheets, pillow

---

[2] Central Agency for the Reception of Asylum Seekers.

covers and hygiene items, and they assigned us rooms. One of the most important pieces of information that we received was about food, namely that it would be provided every morning between 10am and 12pm and that this would be the only distribution for the entire day. While we were moving towards our room with our heavy luggage in our hands and on our shoulders, we were really hit with the feeling of being displaced people.

We were assigned our room. Despite all the information given about the room and building, it was still difficult to find our exact room. After asking some people, we finally reached it. After seeing four beds, four cupboards, four chairs, a table and a fridge in our room, we understood immediately that this room was for only one family – our family! The accommodation arrangements were different from Ter Apel, which gave us a sense of joy, happiness, relief and privacy.

This room was situated on the ground floor and was neat, bright and airy. Our building was surrounded by plants, trees and grass, which we would come to realise produced mosquitoes in summer. Our room had two big windows, but without screens or curtains, so the mosquitoes could easily come inside, creating a problem for sleeping. Many times, we would wake up and kill the mosquitoes with our shoes. The other problem was that people could easily peek inside our room, and sometimes that disturbed our privacy. Therefore, in place of curtains, we hung the bed sheets on the windows. It gave us a sense that necessity truly is the mother of invention.

On the ground floor, there was one communal kitchen with four microwaves, but no cooker. We used to get frozen food every morning from the COA. The taste of the food was completely different from our tastes, but we still ate it, giving thanks to God and remembering those people in the world who don't have anything to eat.

In our building, the toilets and bathrooms were also communal. During our stay, once a week some workers from a cleaning company would come to take care of the general cleanliness of the bathroom and kitchen, but it was not enough. Unfortunately, people were not using them (or maintaining them) how they were supposed to be, and the same situation occurred with the corridors and kitchen. For a couple of days, things were similar in that nobody was taking action towards cleanliness or keeping things in good order. All the people who were living there had nothing to do and were just eating and sleeping. Even the teenagers were living an inactive lifestyle, because their school did not begin until 13th October.

Several times, we discussed this bad situation regarding cleanliness within our family, and at last we came up with the idea of taking steps to address the problem. We thought of this place as our home and we wanted to take care of it and to keep the environment clean. We also remembered what Psalm 89:11 says: 'The heavens are yours, and yours also the earth.' We put this idea into practice and started cleaning, dividing the work among the four of us. One of us went to clean the bathrooms while the other three cleaned the toilet, corridor and kitchen.

Many people appreciated our work. We continued this for several days without asking for help from others. After a while, people started realising that they should also take part in this work of cleanliness. So, everybody was completely involved and, in the end, we made a roster and divided the work among all the people living in that building and it started to look neat and tidy.

Our small initiative of work and action made a specific contribution to the creation of a new and clean environment. This brought a change in the mindset of the people. All the residents started to see things with new eyes and to have a new approach. They started to look after things in a good way. Their response gave us strength and support to go further with other practical activities. By taking this small initiative, we learned to be practical and helpful.

Chapter Four
Interaction

As time went by, we adapted well to life in the camp, but our hearts and souls were still attached to the life we had left behind: our jobs, colleagues, house, relatives, culture, dress, food and, above all, our country. The place where we were born, brought up, studied and got married, and where our children were born was – and is – not easy to forget. We still remember and miss it a lot. All these things had a depressing effect on us. We used to cry many times a day when we thought of these things.

When we arrived in that camp, we were the only Pakistani people. We had noticed, on arrival, that people used to look for their fellow countrymen and women when the buses with new people arrived. We started doing the same, to look for some people who talked in our language, but we never saw any Pakistani people. So we used to help others with their luggage and return, disappointed, to our room.

These circumstances were making us weaker and more depressed day by day. So, we decided that the place where we were living now, with others, was our society, our community, our family – and we had to go forth with them in unity. At that moment, we recalled the universal prayer of unity, said by Jesus in John 17:21: that 'all of them may be one'. We prayed and asked for strength from God in order to develop unity and fraternity among all the people who were living in that place.

We promised each other that we would not cry any more and would not miss all those things that we had left behind. We had to accept these people: our brothers and sisters around us. Even if they had different nationalities, different religions, different ways of living, languages and cultures, there was one thing that we had in common – as human beings, we are all made 'in the image of God' (see Genesis 1:27).

The next morning, we woke up with new ambitions and views of life. We started to greet every person we saw enthusiastically and with a big smile. We felt more energetic and livelier. There was a primary school, but no school for teenagers at the beginning of our time there. So teenagers had nothing to learn and wasted their time gossiping and smoking. Most of the children couldn't speak English; they spoke their own languages.

We were all able to speak good English. Our children decided to gather different groups of teenagers in our building and teach them the basics of the English language in an informal way. We also helped our children in that activity. Many people were pleased with this act of love and kindness. We were also cheerful that our time passed in a good way and that God gave us an opportunity to love everyone, as Jesus said in John 13:34-35: 'A new command I give you: love one another. As I have loved you, so you must love one another. By this everyone will know that you are my disciples, if you love one another.'

We wanted to spend this time in a better way. We went to the COA and asked them for some information about the library. They gave us some information about the library, which was located in Maarheeze. It was almost three kilometres away from the camp. We walked there and asked the librarian for some help in finding some material to learn the Dutch language. We had no library membership or registration cards. Therefore, we could not bring any books back to the camp. We asked the librarian if she could help us read the Dutch words and text.

The librarian was so kind and cooperative. She taught us the alphabet, the days of the week, parts of the body, and some basic vocabulary. Very often, we asked anybody who came in the library for help with how to pronounce a word. At the beginning, it was very difficult for us to utter the words in the way that Dutch people pronounce them. When we pronounced the words, they often laughed. Mostly, people in the library helped us, although sometimes they were too busy with their own activities.

We used to go to the library once a week. We made a vocabulary list and the rest of the week we learned the words by heart as homework. In the camp we asked mostly for help in language learning from any person from the COA who passed by our room, and sometimes we ran after them when they came out from their office or workplace. We found them always cooperative in this regard. We also made requests for help to the security officer who was present in the building at night-time.

It was a small step that we took in order to interact with the people who were living there. This interaction helped us to develop community, fraternity and connections with one another on a small scale. This caused a change in the environment surrounding us and gave us a chance to begin community life.

Chapter Five
Solidarity and Harmony

We really tried to understand the value of interaction and put it into practice in our daily lives. This interaction created the atmosphere of solidarity and harmony among us. We were living in a camp with diverse religious beliefs and backgrounds, but the solidarity and harmony promoted good relations between people of different faiths. We saw an exemplary and visible solidarity on the Muslim feast of Eid al-Adha, which was on 4th October 2014.

Before that feast, the residents of our building made sure there was a general cleanliness inside and outside the building. We formed groups in order to take part in the cleaning work. The women and girls cleaned the rooms, kitchen and corridors, while the men and boys cleaned the toilets and bathrooms and garden area. Working together was a sign of solidarity and harmony. It was preparing to move towards the feast of Eid al-Adha with unity.

We had a good understanding of solidarity and harmony and what they really mean. The involvement of young people and families helped us to promote friendly relationships with each other. We believe this sort of learning is necessary, both for better interfaith relations and for the maturing of one's own beliefs.

On the day of the feast, many people were missing their family members, relatives and friends who were left behind in their home countries. They were remembering them with grief. It is a tradition in Asian countries to invite folk to celebrate Eid together. This is called an Eid Milan Party. The people were really missing this sort of gathering and celebration.

We came from a dreadful situation and were still afraid. Because of all these uncertainties, it was not very easy for us to arrange such parties or celebrations. But we tried to overcome our feelings and did our best to be one with everyone. We left our pessimistic thoughts behind and moved forward into being unified with all the people around us.

We thought, 'What can we do for them at this moment? How can we bring some happiness on this special day?' We made a plan for an Eid Milan Party. We prepared our room and gave it a look of celebration. Our daughter, Nimra, made some Eid wishes cards and placed them in the room. We also learned some Arabic words for greeting during Eid. Then we invited some Muslim friends, families and children for coffee in our room. We gave some candies and toffees to the children. Being a small group, we shared the happiness with one another.

The people who came were so happy and for some moments they forgot their worries and troubles. This get-together proved to be not only a source of commonality, but also a source of joy and delight. This feast became a feast of friendship and solidarity. It helped us to promote social harmony among us. By celebrating this feast, a series of new relationships was born and we realised that there really are differences in our ways of thinking, our traditions and cultures; but while we may have different beliefs, these people are all to be welcomed with respect and love.

Chapter Six
The Environment

It is very important to understand the environment of a camp. It has a certain culture and social context that influences people's lives. The environment of the camp is completely different from the environment of any city, town or village.

While we were there, the children and young teenagers went to school and they remained busy in their school activities. But the people who were older than eighteen years lived an inactive life. Their major 'work' was eating, sleeping, walking, smoking, using the internet, drinking, gossiping and chatting. They were not allowed to work without positive status and a work permit. The majority of the people belonging to this group went to bed very late at night and awoke at midday.

These people played cards late at night and sometimes they would smoke in their rooms. Because of this, the fire alarm was often activated. The guards would come to the rooms and ask everyone who was sleeping to leave at once.

Even small children and old people were not allowed to stay inside. Sometimes it rained and was very cold at night and we had to go outside so that the guards could investigate the cause of the fire alarm going off. It was very difficult to stay outside on those cold nights. Just because of one person, many people had to suffer. We had to face these types of incidents many times.

In the camp there was also a small medical centre. If anyone got sick – for instance, if they caught the flu, or had a cough or a fever – they went to that centre. There was one interesting thing: the people from Middle Eastern countries were used to taking medicine even if they got a headache! In the camp, the nurses gave no medicine for cough, flu or fever. They used to say that you should go and drink cold water and eat ice cream. It was really irritating! We thought that they didn't care about our health, but now we know that they were right. Our bodies have enough immunity to counter these infections.

There were only two places where Wi-Fi was available. The first one was in the security office (run by Trigion) and the other one was in the COA office. There were also signals outside those buildings. People used to gather around those places and call their relatives and friends. It was almost like a call centre! One could hear many different languages there. If there was bad, rainy weather and it was cold, then people would go there with umbrellas, blankets and plastic sheets and hide behind the buildings to be protected against the heavy winds and rain.

There was a place next to the reception areas where there were two information boards. These boards were used to hang lists with the names of people who had post or people who were going to be transferred to another camp for their interviews with the Immigratie- en Naturalisatiedienst (IND).[3] These lists were hung twice a day. People were always hopeful that their names would be on the transfer list. Their happiness was dependent upon it. If someone's name was on that list they would return with pleasure after seeing it, while those whose names were not there returned sadly to their rooms.

In reality, the people had no role to play. They lived unimportant and unnoticeable lives in the camp. It was considered that the basic needs, such as shelter, food and medicine, were enough for refugees. But life is really more than those things. The experience of living in a camp is and was an experience of inability and insignificance.

In our lives, when we are neglected and become 'unimportant', I believe we can view it as a sign that we are being chosen to share this experience with others. We can experience the presence of God in our weakness: 'He has performed mighty deeds with his arm; he has scattered those who are proud in their inmost thoughts. He has brought down rulers from their thrones but has lifted up the humble. He has filled the hungry with good things but has sent the rich away empty' (Luke 1:51-53). God does not only reveal Himself in extraordinary places or events and important people. The same God also reveals Himself among common, simple, 'unimportant' people, places and events of life. God is above all the geographical and environmental conditions. He is beyond social and cultural structures.

---

[3] Immigration and Naturalisation Service.

We gradually learned in this environment what encouragement, support, help, sharing and taking care of each other really meant. For us, the atmosphere of this place seemed silent and contemplative. We discovered that in taking the opportunity to make an experience a spiritual one, getting involved in community life, time is never wasted. This was truly an experience of trusting in God's provision and in His generosity and grace. God's grace is greater than human weaknesses, fears and limitations. He is interested in our personal circumstances and He shows His concern and care for us.

Chapter Seven
Work of Mercy

With the change of season and the arrival of winter, the COA decided to give warm clothes to all the people. They came up with a plan to distribute the clothes, distributing tokens per building. The first building they started with was ours. After receiving the tokens, we thought about what we could contribute to this activity. With these thoughts going on in our minds, we headed towards the COA office and asked the staff about doing some volunteer work with them in this regard.

Our proposal about volunteer work for the arrangement and distribution of warm clothes among the people was welcomed by the COA. They gave us the responsibility of working two or three times a week at the clothes store. This was a huge activity; one big building was devoted to this work.

So many people from Budel brought warm clothes and shoes for the refugees. The COA staff received them, and we placed and arranged all the clothes and shoes according to gender and size in different rooms. The rooms looked like shops, full of shoes and garments.

Anyone who came there to get warm clothes and shoes had thirty minutes for choosing the things according to their preference and size. There were fitting rooms available for their final choice. If someone found the clothes did not fit them, we gave them another garment to try, and we did this with great interest and love. Many times, we encouraged them that this colour, shirt or trousers suited them well. By this act of love, we garnered everybody's liking and fondness. It was a really friendly atmosphere there. We worked with great dedication and passion, carrying out this service with all our heart and soul.

We found, many times, that people did not show interest in volunteer work – work that is done without payment. But we regarded this social work as a service, as a commitment and as a responsibility. We did the volunteer work under the light of Christianity. We used to do volunteer and social work for a long time in church activities in our own country. For us, to be a volunteer is like the rebirth of the society of the early believers. They were committed Christians. They served and helped others everywhere.

Every time we came back from the work, we had a feeling of satisfaction. We discovered that this work gave us much peace and joy. We believed that in doing this, we served God in humanity: 'Whatever you do, work at it with all your heart, as working for the Lord, not for human masters' (Colossians 3:23).

We strongly believe that we are called to live out Matthew 25:35-36: 'For I was hungry and you gave me something to eat, I was thirsty and you gave me something to drink, I was a stranger and you invited me in, I needed clothes and you clothed me, I was ill and you looked after me, I was in prison and you came to visit me.'

This was our secret to volunteering: doing the work with the gospel in mind.

The spirituality of this vocation comes from the gospel and it becomes visible in society though works of mercy and charity. We find maturity in our vocation when we please God through serving others. We find God by loving and serving others; we were involved in this volunteer work in order to love and serve others. Some people were attracted by this simple example and work. Through this activity, we drew others and involved some other people in the work. The COA gratefully acknowledged our volunteer work and gave us a certificate of appreciation. We felt proud to be volunteers, even in the darkest period of our lives.

52

Chapter Eight
Once Again to Ter Apel

With the passing of time, we engaged ourselves in different activities. All the people who had come with us to Budel from Ter Apel were being transferred one by one for their interview with the IND. We used to go to see those families off and helped them to carry their luggage to the bus or departure point. While saying farewell, tears came into our eyes because we had built up friendly relationships with each other. So, we had tearful partings; we deeply valued the time we had spent together.

This went on until almost all the families we knew there had been transferred. We were left behind. When everyone was gone, we experienced feelings of loneliness and sadness. We used to go twice a day to check if our names were on the transfer list. When our names were not found on the list, we returned, bitterly disappointed. But we wished success to those people who left for their interview with the IND. There were no apparent criteria for being transferred. Many people stayed in Budel for a month or two, and were then transferred to the next place, where the interview was going to be conducted. But there were also people like us who waited for their transfer for more than three or four months.

One Sunday we were coming back from the church and, as we entered the camp, we went to see the transfer list, but there was no list displayed on the board yet. Once again, we came back to our room with a feeling of frustration. Around 3pm a girl came rushing into our room and told us that there was a new transfer list. We went to see if our names were there or not. Our names were there! That made us smile.

The next day, at 12.00, we were about to depart. We had a short time to get ready and to prepare our luggage for the next camp. We went to the COA to collect our transfer documents and extended our greetings to them, thanking them for all their kind service and cooperation. We had mixed feelings because we had been in Budel for three months; living there had given us a feeling of home and community spirit. Now, we had feelings of displacement and dislocation again.

In Budel, the school for teenagers had begun in the middle of October. Our children went to school for three weeks. In this school, they learned some vocabulary and how to ask for basic information in the Dutch language. In the class, the teachers provided them with different situations where they used the vocabulary in simple and systematic ways. In a short time, they gained an understanding of a few words of Dutch. After school, they tried to teach us what they had learned.

After finding out about the transfer, they went to their school and told their teachers and classmates. The news of the transfer came as a shock to the teachers, who were impressed by their learning attitude in class. The teachers gave them a very nice report for the three weeks in which they had studied. After taking those reports, our children said goodbye to their teachers and fellow students. Although we were all pleased to be moving on, the children were very sad about saying farewell to their friends.

On our last night in Budel, we had dinner with a young Pakistani couple who had come to the camp just three weeks before our departure. After dinner, they helped us pack our luggage. They were very sad about our transfer. The next morning, they helped us with taking our luggage to the bus.

On 10th November 2014 around 12.00, we left for Ter Apel. When we were about to leave, two members of the COA staff came to say goodbye and pay their respects to us for our help and volunteer work. They wished us success for our future and the interview process.

So, we were transferred to Ter Apel once again. We recalled all those moments we had spent there.

Chapter Nine
Patience

The closer we got to Ter Apel, the more memories came back to us of the days spent there before. While we were still on our way, we were thinking about whether we would go to the same accommodation or somewhere else. When we reached the camp, our bus dropped us off in front of different buildings from before. The COA staff welcomed us and took us to our room.

It was freezing cold in that room. At first glance, we were shocked and surprised to see it. We felt terribly sad. Our room was too small for four people. There were four cupboards, a small table with four chairs and there were four beds which were placed on top of each other. There was no free movement even for two people. It was really a narrow passage, where only one person could walk at a time.

We were also hungry, as we had eaten nothing. Here, there were specific times for breakfast, lunch and dinner. We had missed our lunch and had to wait till dinner time.

When it was time for dinner, we went out and saw a big line of people standing outside the dining hall. We stood for an hour to get in there.

When we got inside, we were given bread and soup to eat. We ate very little and then returned to our room. In the dining hall, if someone, after eating their own food, wished for more to eat, they had to wait till everybody had eaten, then afterwards the COA could serve them the remaining food. If somebody wanted extra food, they had to wait for an hour.

We could only eat food in the dining room and weren't allowed to take it into our rooms. If we felt hungry during other parts of the day, we couldn't eat anything. A van used to draw up outside the camp to sell food items, but we usually couldn't buy anything to eat because we didn't have enough money. When sometimes we were able to buy something, we had no plates, knives or forks to eat it with.

It was cold in Ter Apel and our small room was very cold. We turned on the central heating, but still it was cold. We got blankets from the COA, but they weren't enough to protect us against that chilly weather. Because of all the travelling and hunger, we all got headaches. There was an electric kettle in our room, but we didn't have any coffee or teabags. Nasreen went to the COA reception area and asked if they could give us coffee and teabags. They gave us some and so we drank coffee to warm ourselves up and relax.

Living in these miserable conditions, at this new place, nobody was talking on that first night before going to sleep. All of a sudden, I came up with an idea to change the situation. I started telling the other family members the story of the birth of Jesus: how Jesus, when He was born, had no proper shelter, how He and His family had to stay in a stable on that night.

After telling the whole story, everyone remembered that Mary and Joseph were calm and happy in spite of all the difficulties. This story gave us a new strength and we became positive and motivated. We decided that we should be thankful to God that we didn't have to stay in a stable; we had a roof over our heads, clothes to wear, food to eat and a place to sleep. Afterwards, we prayed together as we always did, and the atmosphere within the room changed; all that sadness disappeared.

The morning after our arrival, our children started going to school. This school was situated in the camp and its name was Internationale SchakelKlas.[4] On the first day, we went with our children to see the school and to fill out the admission forms. The reports that were given by the previous teachers were shown to the administrators of the school. They were very happy after reading them! Our children did the admission tests and then the decisions were made about which classes they would be in. In this school, they studied subjects such as the Dutch language, maths, English, science, creative art, health and physical education.

The following day, we decided to live as we did in Budel. The buildings needed to be clean, because the living area was so crowded. The bathrooms here were small and people didn't use them properly. They used to throw

---

[4] A school for children who speak little or none of the Dutch language – abbreviated to ISK. This provides international language transition classes.

bottles and disposable glasses into the toilets. Some people, after taking a bath, left the shampoo and soap wrappers on the floor. Some of the staff did come to clean up once a day, but the bathrooms didn't stay clean because so many people used them. We began to keep the area where we lived clean and slowly others also joined us.

Our room was located in the corner of the building, near the main entrance. The people normally went outside the building to smoke, but when it was cold and rainy weather, a large group of women sat inside, in the corridor near our room, smoking the hookah[5] and chatting till midnight. Even though they opened the main entrance door to send the smoke outside, they did not fully succeed. Therefore, a lot of smoke entered our room. Their smoke and noise were creating a disturbance for us.

This situation led to anger, stress and frustration, because our rights were being violated. But we displayed patience towards them by remembering that patience is one of the characteristics of a Christian. We were 'fixing our eyes on Jesus, the pioneer and perfecter of faith. For the joy that was set before him he endured the cross, scorning its shame, and sat down at the right hand of the throne of God' (Hebrews 12:2).

---

[5] An instrument used for smoking tobacco and, sometimes, cannabis or opium. The vapour passes through a basin of water, usually made of glass, and is then inhaled.

Chapter Ten
The Lord Watches

After spending two weeks in Ter Apel, we received a letter for an appointment with a lawyer for legal aid. The aim of this meeting was to prepare us for the interview procedure with IND. This appointment was an indication that our interview procedure was about to start. As we read the letter, we were a bit nervous because we had never met a lawyer before in our lives. We had no idea how the meeting would be conducted and what sort of questions they would ask us. Still, we were praying, and we gave all of our worries into God's hands with this strong belief: 'The LORD watches over the strangers' (Psalm 146:9, NRSV).

Our appointment was on 26th November 2014, so we got up early in the morning as it was a rule to report to the reception area at 8am, even if your appointment would be held during the early or late afternoon. We had the meeting with the lawyer scheduled for 2pm, but we were present at the main reception area of the IND at 7am. It took a lot of time for them to bring people inside, with many inspections and security clearances.

As we reached the reception area, we saw that people were already gathered outside. It was foggy, windy and cold weather and the reception area was quite small. Therefore, only six to seven people could go inside at a time and the rest had to stand outside in the freezing cold. So the people who were standing outside formed a line and went in, one by one. There were a few families that came and stood after us with their small children so we did an act of love and gave them our place. Though it was bitterly cold, we had a joy in our hearts that we had helped the small children, in preventing them from standing longer in the cold.

Finally, after waiting for such a long time for security clearance, we went to the main building where we were supposed to wait for our lawyer. They had a typical Dutch name, so we had no idea if our lawyer was male or female. We were staring at every lawyer who passed by. Time passed, and then at 2pm a female lawyer called out our names and we thanked God that after waiting so long we knew who our lawyer was.

She took us to a room with an interpreter and introduced herself. As she was so gentle and kind, the feeling of nervousness that we had in our hearts went away just a few minutes after meeting her. She briefed us about our further procedure and gave us legal advice regarding our case. After a long conversation, the meeting ended on a good note and we came back to our room around 4pm.

We had heard that people who were ahead of us in the procedure used to sit up for long nights preparing for the interview with the IND, like they would for a high-school exam. When we saw those people, we thought that the interview would be quite difficult, as it was the most important stage of the whole procedure. We also prepared late into the night for our interviews, and were quite worried, with a feeling of fear in our hearts.

On 2nd December the time came for our first interview with the IND regarding our identity, nationality and travel route. The procedure for entering the IND building was the same. We got up early in the morning and reported at the reception area. We were seated in a waiting hall where, one by one, the employees of the IND and the interpreters came and took all the people who were present there for their interviews. As it was an individual interview, we were taken separately into different rooms. In the evening, the four of us shared with each other that the interviews had been conducted in a good atmosphere.

The process goes like this: after the interview with the IND, asylum seekers take the interview report to a lawyer, who reads it to them. If there is a need to correct or add to it due to misunderstandings in translation during the interview, then the lawyer indicates this in the report. So, the next day, 3rd December, we were sent a report of the interview. Together with our lawyer, we were able to correct it and then send it to the IND. We also needed further legal advice regarding our second interview, which was to be specifically about our case.

The following day was the date of our second and most important interview regarding the problem for which we had left our country. This interview went well too, and the next day we went again to our lawyer. Alongside some clarifications, she told us about our further procedure and said that we needed to come again on 9th December, as that would be our decision day. As instructed by our lawyer, we came on that day to receive the decision made by the IND. We found out that the IND had made a decision to send us for the 'extended' asylum procedure.

It was a sad moment for us when we realised that we needed to follow the extended procedure, but at the same time we strongly trusted in God, who takes care of our worries in every situation of our lives. As Peter says in his first letter: 'Cast all your anxiety on him because he cares for you' (1 Peter 5:7).

Chapter Eleven
Tears of Happiness

On the evening of 10th December 2014, when we went for dinner in the dining hall, we saw that there was a paper with our names on it. It was a transfer letter. We were being transferred to a new camp in Pagedal, which was not far from Ter Apel. At first, we became worried. We thought that it would be the same as Ter Apel. It was a place where we were supposed to stay for a long time, and that's why we were worried – how would we live in this kind of environment for long? In this new camp, we would get money to cook our own food. We were happy about that; at least we were going to be able to eat the food that we liked!

We packed our things. The next morning the people who were being transferred were called by the COA and told about their new locations. We left Ter Apel and reached Pagedal at midday. When we went to the reception area, COA staff welcomed us and gave us a money card. They told us that we could get money from the 'Centrum'. One of the COA staff led us to our new home.

We were amazed to see it. It was a very beautiful house. It reminded us of our own house back in Pakistan. Since we had arrived in the Netherlands, we had never been in a house; we had always stayed in one room. The first thing we did was to thank God. We went inside and prayed to God about the lovely house. It was nothing less than a dream. It was nothing like what we had expected. We believed God had rewarded us for our patience!

The house was big and we had nothing to do there – no work, no cleaning – because it was already very neat and clean. Everything was organised. We had only two bags of clothes, which we put in the cupboard. We were so happy. We watched TV, sat on the sofa and got excited about everything! We were so glad, we forgot about food! We had eaten nothing, but we felt no hunger.

At 3pm, Aroon and I went to the Centrum to get the money and to buy some crockery and groceries. But there was some problem with the activation of the money card. We called Nasreen, and asked her to go to reception in inform the COA about the card. We had no mobile phone, just a tablet, but we had put a Sim card in that. When someone called on it, everyone could hear, because we had no headphones! Nasreen asked somebody to talk to me on the tablet. The COA staff member laughed but, at Nasreen's request, talked to me about the activation of the card. But the problem was not solved. Therefore, she gave Nasreen €30 to buy food. My son and I collected the money, walking through rain with no umbrella; then we bought some crockery, chicken, rice and vegetables.

Nasreen and Nimra cooked the meal. They spent a long time on it and were so pleased while cooking. The smell of the food spread throughout the house. Everyone was so excited because we were about to taste our own food after four months. It was an amazing feeling. When the food was ready, we put everything on the dining table. We prayed before eating and thanked God for that moment.

When we started eating, tears came to our eyes and we started crying. At the time, we didn't know whether they were tears of joy or sorrow. In fact, they were tears of happiness. We still remember those times. We will always treasure those moments: they were moments of joy, happiness and delight. For a time, we forgot all about the suffering that we had had to face in the past few months.

We lived like this for a few days. But we really missed one thing and that was the interaction that we had experienced with people in Budel and Ter Apel.

In Pagedal it was really quiet and we could hardly see people passing by. After five days, two people from the COA came to our house and told us that we would be transferred again, this time to Katwijk. It was a shock for us. But they told us that these houses in Pagedal were used for holidays, therefore staying there was too expensive and they couldn't pay for everything.

We were very depressed about leaving that beautiful place. But we accepted it as the will of God. We thought, 'God has His own plans for us. We shouldn't be disappointed any more over it.'

Chapter Twelve
Delight

On 15th December, the COA came to us and told us that we were going to be transported to Katwijk at 8am the next day. We packed our things again. The next morning, the COA came and checked everything. We had cleaned the whole house with love and affection because it had given us happiness; we had become attached to that house in a period of just a few days. We handed over the keys to the COA and went outside. It was bitterly cold.

Our bus didn't arrive on time; because of some problem, it was two hours late. We all had to stand outside with our bags and wait for the bus in front of the COA's reception area.

There was no shelter. We had normal shoes, not winter boots. Our hands and feet were freezing. We were hiding behind a wall to try to protect ourselves from the cold. There was no place to sit; people were sitting on their bags. After some time, the COA realised what was happening and then they brought coffee for us. Everyone rushed to get the coffee; people just wanted to be warm. After two hours, the bus arrived and everyone hurried towards it. After a few minutes, we left Pagedal for Katwijk.

We left Pagedal feeling curious about our new destination. We had had a very nice time in Pagedal. It felt like home there and it had given us happiness after a long time. We were busy in our own thoughts when one of the passengers went to the driver and asked him to stop the bus because he wanted to go to the toilet. He could only speak Arabic and, at first, the driver didn't understand what he said, but then some people translated for him.

The driver seemed frightened about why the man was asking him to stop the bus. The man kept asking the driver to stop, but the driver wouldn't. He said that he was not allowed to, and would only stop at Katwijk. People were laughing at the man who wanted to go to the toilet, but I think they were also feeling pity for him.

When we arrived in Katwijk, everyone was looking for the COA flag . At last we arrived – it had taken three hours of travelling. We got our luggage and one of the COA staff took us inside a building; then one of the workers showed us our room. The buildings were newly built and some were still under construction. It was very muddy and it was also raining, so it was not a very good scene; we felt quite petrified.

We went to our room. We were not happy as we were back in one room. It was a small room for four people to live in.

After a while, I went out to ask someone for information about the shop so that I could buy something for dinner. Somebody took me to a shop where I bought some vegetables, chicken and spices. I bought cabbage, and then found out it wasn't cabbage! We cooked it and, while eating, realised it was salad leaves. In our country, cabbage looked like that, so naturally we thought it was cabbage! We laughed a lot about that.

After eating, we put our things in the cabinets and also rearranged our room. It was an exhausting day, and we were disappointed that we had to stay in one room again. We were tired, we prayed, and we went to sleep.

The building where we lived had two floors. On each floor, there were thirteen apartments, one kitchen for ninety-one people and one room for laundry. Each apartment had two rooms: one room for four people and the other room for three people. In every apartment, there was one shared bathroom and toilet.

Our room was located on the first floor. It had two glass windows: one was permanently closed and another one could be opened in order to get fresh air. At the back of our room, there were plants and beautiful fields covered with grass, where all day sheep, horses and cows were seen grazing. Along with animals, there were also some beautiful birds, especially seabirds, in the fields.

This charming view took us very close to nature. Nature is one of God's beautiful creations. 'Through him all things were made; without him nothing was made that has been made' (John 1:3). This view of nature was a great source of delight, especially at that time when we were so disappointed.

Chapter Thirteen
The Church

The next day we went to the COA information office to ask about the children's schooling. They said that, because of Christmas, school work would start after the holidays. We also asked about a school for adults, but they said that only people who had been granted a residence permit could go to school and learn the Dutch language officially. People like us had to wait till their procedure was completed with IND. So we were disappointed.

It was the Advent season; we were approaching Christmas. We were very sad because we were away from our homeland, friends and family. We used to celebrate Christmas with our relatives and friends. Here, it was nothing like it used to be back at home. It was so simple: no new clothes, no celebration, no get-together, no air of festivity, no picnic, no cousins and relatives to have fun with. We missed everything. Before Christmas, some people from Interkerkelijk Werkgroep

Asielzoekerscentrum Katwijk (IWAK)[6] came to give some to all the refugees.

One of the volunteers came to our room and he gave us four large Christmas presents, which were wrapped very beautifully. When he left the room, Nimra and Aroon immediately opened them. They were shouting with joy and happiness.

We are Christians, so we wanted to go to church. One day I went out looking for a Catholic church and, by asking people, at last we found Parochiekern H Joannes de Doper in Katwijk. Every Sunday and on other religious feasts, we went there to attend Holy Mass. For the first couple of months, we walked to church every Sunday morning, even in rough weather. From the camp it took thirty minutes to reach the church.

After attending the Holy Mass on Sunday, we immediately came back to the camp because we did not know the members of the congregation. Nobody knew us, who we were or where we came from. In our culture, when the Holy Mass ends on Sunday, people mostly talk for a long time outside the church about all sorts of things: family matters, job issues, politics, church activities and current national and international issues. But we found the Dutch culture completely different in this regard.

On one Saturday after the Holy Mass, I went to pray in front of the tabernacle. Meanwhile some members of the committee were preparing to close up the church. One of them was waiting for me to finish the prayer. As I finished, the man asked me, 'Who are you and where do you come

---

[6] Interdenominational group/team involved with asylum seekers.

from?' He also introduced himself to me as Marten van der Meer. Gradually, he became our friend, and he introduced us to Father Michel Hagen who is parish priest of Parochie H Augustinus. So, in this way, we got involved in parish life.

Another milestone was Palm Sunday, 29th March 2015. When we walked to church it was nice weather, but when the Holy Mass ended it was raining. Everyone went back to their homes by car or bike, but we were left behind. After waiting a long time for the rain to stop, I went to the parish office to ask someone if they could lend us some umbrellas. Then I met Jan, a sacristan, who said he could take us back to the camp in his car.

As we travelled, Jan asked us about ourselves and we told him about our situation. He asked how we travelled to church, and we told him that we walked. He said that he could come to pick us up on Sundays to bring us to the church and would give us a lift back if it was raining. After some time, he talked to Erna Geurts, the lady who provided the transport service that helped older people who wished to come to church. They decided to take turns to come and pick us up if the weather was bad.

Later, Jan talked to the other parishioners about us and they got us some bikes. We felt so grateful for their strong act of love in our needy situation. But the problem was that Nasreen and Nimra couldn't ride the bikes because, in our country, women generally never do! My son and I taught them to ride, but it was difficult. Nimra learned a bit more quickly than Nasreen. But then, after one month, both of them were able to cycle.

At the beginning of April 2015, Marten gave me an article that had been published in *Missio Nieuwsbrief Maart* in the Netherlands. It was news about the recent terrorist attack on two churches in Youhanabad, Lahore, in Pakistan. I contacted the Missio office in Den Haag (The Hague), in order to offer help. On 19th May 2015, the coordinator invited me to the Missio office, so we could get to know one another. Later on, she invited me to write an article about the children of Pakistan, pertaining to their activities in the Holy Childhood Association. Some of the text of the article was published in *Missio Kerk Wereldwijd* September–October 2015.

In the same year, the Missio office arranged a campaign to gather some funds on World Mission Sunday for poor Pakistani Christian children who do not have the chance to get an education. To this end, they arranged a meeting in Sint-Catharinakathedraal in Utrecht on 26th September 2015, where fifty people gathered. I shared with them my pastoral, social and educational experiences, which I had had in Pakistan at parish or diocesan level. This was my contribution: to give some information about the Pakistani Christian community.

On 17th and 18th October 2015, World Mission Sunday was celebrated in Parochiekern H Joannes de Doper in Katwijk. During the Holy Mass, Nimra and Aroon did the Bible reading in the Dutch language for the first time. Some parishioners help them to prepare the reading. Our family prepared this programme with the collaboration of some parishioners.

During our stay in Katwijk, we were invited to attend other churches as well, where I and Nasreen spoke about the situation of Christians in Pakistan.

On 24th December, there was a Christmas Brunch, which was organised by the local churches at Kerkhaventje Katwijk. Almost 250 people from the camp in Katwijk participated in the feast. Although the people were gathered there from different nations, cultures, customs and languages, they looked so united. There was a profound and visible harmony among them. The people sang Christmas songs in Arabic, English, Persian, Dutch and so on. We also sang in the Urdu language. Christmas Brunch became a feast of fraternity, a feast of peace, a feast of harmony, and a feast of solidarity and love.

On Saturday 26th March 2016, in the afternoon, IWAK organised a Paasfeest[7] at the chapel located in 1e Mientlaan-Katwijk, where 200 people gathered from the camp. We gave our help to IWAK in cleaning and preparing the place, and also in the preparation and distribution of food. By working together, we experienced true harmony and community. On this occasion, Easter songs were sung and a special Easter message was given. The Paasfeest ended with a delicious meal.

On 17th June 2016, some volunteers from Katwijk arranged Sing and Share evening at the Kerkhaventje bij de Oude Kerk aan de Boulevard. A small group of people from the camp went to this event. We also participated in this get-together: we presented Christian songs and shared with other participants. There were also people from

---

[7] An Easter feast.

China, Vietnam, Syria, Iran and Afghanistan who shared and sang songs. By participating in this beautiful event, we tried to open our hearts and ears to one another. It was truly an atmosphere of love, fraternity and peace.

While living in Katwijk, we carried on these activities at church level because we learned that we can do these things in Jesus, as Paul describes in Philippians 4:13: 'I can do all this through him who gives me strength.'

Chapter Fourteen
Getting Involved

In Katwijk, we got involved in church activities, but we wanted more to do. We did not like living an inactive life at all. We thought about it so much and prayed regularly, asking Jesus to change this idle and passive situation in our lives. The time was passing very slowly.

It was one of the coldest evenings in January 2015, when Nimra and I went shopping in Katwijk. After shopping, and before we came back to our room, we saw two young ladies, who we found out were called Diana and Inge. As they approached us, we introduced ourselves, then we invited them into our room because it was cold outside. offered them coffee. On this visit, they invited Nimra to participate in a meeting that they conducted for girls. They told us their purpose was to visit young girls who live in the camp, and organise some social, sporting and spiritual activities for them. Diana worked with the religious organisation Stichting Gave, and with IWAK.

Nimra accepted their invitation warmly and went to attend the meeting with other girls. It was a nice experience of getting to know others. In their meeting they got a chance to paint candles and decorate cupcakes, and did some other activities. She placed a cross on her candle with the words 'Life is beautiful'. She brought it back to our room. After that, we lit it many times and we sat around it, praying to God to eliminate all the darkness from our lives and make our lives shine with His light.

Diana came to visit us again and we talked about how we had met each other the first time. She and Inge were on their first visit, and they offered their help to Jesus and asked what they could do for Him on that evening in this new place and among these people. As they saw us, they believed Jesus wanted them to visit us that evening. So we all discovered that visit was God's plan.

Later on, Diana used to come to our room and pray with us, and she would share something with us about the love of God. Once she brought along her pastor and we prayed together for peace in the world.

Another day, Diana came to visit us with a friend. She told us about the clothes shop in the chapel at 1e Mientlaan-Katwijk. This chapel was no longer used specifically for church services, but for social activities for refugees under the supervision of IWAK. It was within walking distance from where we were. Every Tuesday, they gave clothes, shoes, toys and other items to people for very low prices and sometimes even free of charge.

One day we decided to go there and we found that the clothes were very cheap and the quality was good. We were so happy that we could buy clothes for nominal prices. The clothes shop was also run by the members of IWAK. Later on, Nasreen started to help every Tuesday as a volunteer in the shop.

I was interested in participating in some of the activities that were conducted in the chapel. Diana and Inge proposed my name to IWAK to volunteer to help Joan Joek, the manager of the chapel. IWAK accepted the proposal and I helped there voluntarily in many ways.

We also found out about the Dutch lessons that took place in the same chapel. Some people conducted the lessons for refugees voluntarily. We started going there, and in that way we came to know many other students and teachers. The teachers prepared the lessons in a simple way, but their presentation was very interesting. It was noticeable that the students came late to the class on so many occasions, but the teachers were always on time. The teachers were so committed and dedicated to their volunteer and educational work.

At first Nasreen had no interest in learning the Dutch language. She used to say, 'What is the use of learning the language until we know what our social status is?' But later on, when we had persuaded her, she joined the classes and really liked them. She never missed her classes! She took part in lots of activities through them. Once her group went to a library in Katwijk, where they got free library passes. Their picture was also in the *Katwijks Nieuwsblad*.

In the classes, not only did they give the lesson, but they also provided the study materials, notebooks, files, pencils and so on. During the break, they even arranged coffee and tea for the students. They created a very interesting and ideal environment for learning.

The teachers helped us to build up a large vocabulary. New words were learned through vocabulary exercises and students were encouraged to apply what they had learned in class. Some lessons started with a grammar section, presenting the basic grammar with examples and sentences. The lessons had exercises to develop grammatical skills and knowledge. The students also had the chance to read and to get help with pronunciation skills, and speaking practice in class was done in a simple way. While giving lessons, each teacher used different approaches with a range of interesting exercises.

Diana introduced us to other volunteers, who conducted sporting activities and presentations for boys who lived in the camp in Katwijk. We helped them in practical ways when they arranged meetings for the boys, sometimes by distributing invitations in the camp. During the meeting we prepared cold drinks, coffee, tea and edible items. The volunteers encouraged boys to get involved in the activities. The boys discovered that playing sport improved fitness levels and increased relationship opportunities.

We used to earnestly pray about how we could get involved with others in our new environment. At this time, we learned that whatever we ask from God in confidence, He hears us and fulfils our desires. As in 1 John 5:14: 'This is the confidence we have in approaching God: that if we ask anything according to his will, he hears us.'

Chapter Fifteen
Education

In January 2015, Nimra and Aroon started going to school in the Internationale Schakelklas in Leiden, where they started to learn the Dutch language properly for higher studies, even though they had already taken some basic lessons.

Between January 2015 and July 2016, they mainly focused on the language lessons up to Nt2 Level (B2). On 28th June 2016, they both passed the national exam in Dutch as a second language (Staatsexamen Nederlands als tweede taal, Programma II) and each got a diploma. Besides this, Nimra studied at VWO 3 and Aroon at HAVO 3 levels. During this period, they took classes for some months in chemistry and physics at Leonardo College, Noachstraat. For the academic year 2016–17, Nimra was promoted to VWO 4 and Aroon to HAVO 4 levels and they were going to study at da Vinci College, Kagerstraat.

At the beginning, it was very difficult for Nasreen and me to understand the education system in the Netherlands.

When Nimra and Aroon told us about the different education levels in the Netherlands it was puzzling; but this was the same for other parents in the camp, too.

Although the education system of the Netherlands was unclear to us, my wife and I began to see noticeable changes occurring in our children's learning; in their character building, confidence, knowledge, personality, thinking and wisdom. Many times, they shared happily with us about the differences they observed in their day-to-day school life. Nimra and Aroon were very intelligent students in Pakistan and, with the guidance of teachers, they soon developed their hidden skills and abilities. So, within a short passage of time, they became extraordinary students.

Nimra was a very shy girl when she came to the Netherlands. But under the guiding hand of her teachers, she developed a lot. In Pakistan she studied for ten years, but never had a chance to present anything in front of the class. Here she had to do many presentations and built a lot of confidence. Besides studying what was on the curriculum, she took part in other activities. She also developed her drawing skills. Aroon grew a lot, too. He also took part in extracurricular activities, such as sports. In Pakistan there are not very many programmes related to sports. Here, he got a chance to develop his skills, as well as improving in his studies.

My wife and I got a chance to meet their children's teachers. Their remarks about their progress were excellent. One of the teachers told us in this meeting that we must be proud of our children. They were doing such hard work and were fully involved in their own progress, even though they were living in such difficult circumstances. They were trying their best to overcome this unfavourable atmosphere and were focusing on their studies. If they got a residence permit, and studied hard with the same passion, we were told they could serve the Netherlands with full devotion and commitment. These comments were unforgettable and very encouraging for us.

During the time we were in the process of applying for the the residence permit with the IND, Nimra was approaching eighteen years of age. We had heard many rumours that children who reached eighteen and had no residence permit didn't get any financial help from the COA regarding their studies. Nimra was very disappointed, displeased and frustrated by all these rumours. She thought that she wouldn't be able to study any further and wouldn't be able to fulfil all her dreams. As a child, she always dreamed of being a doctor. While playing with her dolls, she used to pretend that they were her patients. She would walk around the house with her toy doctor's kit and check our health. She was always concerned about everyone's health! But after all this gossip and the rumours, she was starting to lose hope and was very upset.

She looked gloomy and low-spirited. She went to her class mentor and discussed the whole situation with her. The mentor tried to pacify her and said that she would raise this issue in a meeting and ask the school administration about it. After a few days, the mentor told Nimra that the school had funds for children who faced these situations. So, if the COA stopped the financial help, the school would shoulder all her study expenses. After this, we and Nimra were happy and all felt lighter.

Nasreen and I went to the COA person concerned to discuss Nimra's matter. They told us that the COA would continue to finance her because if somebody is enrolled in an Internationale SchakelKlas before turning eighteen, the COA is responsible for all the study expenses for that person. All the matters were solved in a peaceful way.

By contrast, Aroon could be very irritating at times! He annoyed Nimra a lot. It made him happy! But Nimra told him that he would be sorry for all this when they had their maths test. Aroon was not as good as Nimra in maths, and always needed her help. So, whenever they had tests, she got Aroon to do anything she wanted!

Chapter Sixteen
Stress

As mentioned in other chapters, during the asylum procedure, the applicants have nothing to do.

Our lives were bound to one room. We had no jobs, and had to stay inside in our room for the whole day. Our lives seemed aimless and without any goal. Our children went to school and were studying: their lives were better than ours. They had friends and went out sometimes. Despite all the problems, they found a way to be happy and enjoy themselves.

Life in the camp was not always like this. At the beginning, we thought that all this would be over within a few months, but it didn't happen like that. After our interview with the IND, we were just waiting and that's when all our troubles and worries really began. We had to wait a long while for our decision – two years. All this waiting time led to tension and frustration, which was rooted in depression, trauma and stress.

Within a period of few months, I became very depressed. My family noticed many changes in me. I stayed in bed the whole day, thinking. I didn't answer when someone asked me something, began to eat less, stopped talking, didn't sleep at night, got irritated about small things and didn't shave or comb my hair. My family asked me many times to go to the doctor, but every time they said that, I became angry and said, 'There is nothing wrong with me.' My condition got worse day by day. They thought I looked like a depressed person, but I never agreed to go to the doctor.

One day, Nasreen decided to go to our COA contact person. She went there, started crying and said nothing. The contact person asked her, 'What happened? Why are you crying?' and Nasreen said two words: 'Help me.' Then he asked her to be calm and tell the whole story. She told him about my condition and that I wouldn't go to the doctor, even though my condition was worsening day by day. The contact person assured her that he would come to the room and talk to me.

After some time, he came to the room and saw me. He was shocked. He said, 'Javed, you have become very weak. You don't look like the same person we met a few months ago.' He advised me to visit a doctor, but I refused and claimed to be healthy. But still he kept on trying to convince me.

In the end I agreed to pay a visit to the doctor and the COA person immediately made an appointment for the next day. The doctor talked with me and gave me tablets to help me sleep, as well as antidepressants. Because of this sickness, the atmosphere had become very depressing and sad in our room, but still the family kept strong.

While my condition was not good, the children couldn't concentrate on their studies, so we asked COA staff repeatedly to give us in addition the other room in our apartment, because it was empty at that time. But they refused and it got very difficult for us to handle everything in one room.

After the medicines started working, I felt a little better and became involved in different activities in IWAK. I went there from my Dutch lessons but I still felt I wasn't doing enough. I wanted to do more, because the more time I spent in the camp, the more depressed I became. At last, I met Mr Jan van de Plas in the chapel. He invited me to come to the public lecture in Vrije Universiteit in Amsterdam. These public lectures were on peace, justice, trauma and religion and were organised by Dr Fernando Enns. During this series of public lectures, Jan gave me an idea – to apply to study in Vrije Universiteit. I liked this idea and finally was admitted to this university to do a Master's in Theology and Religious Studies: Peace, Trauma and Religion.

As I recovered, Nasreen was becoming depressed. After seeing what had happened to me, and because of the circumstances, she couldn't help but feel sad. This sadness plunged her into darkness. She was getting into the same state as I had been – or even worse. She didn't want to see her children or believe in God. She said if He was here and listening to us, why would He let us go through all these bad situations? Her illness got worse day by day. She had nightmares and wouldn't sleep or let us turn the lights off. Nothing we did was helping.

After a week of this, she was very depressed. At one stage, she said she would prefer to die. I asked her to go to the doctor, and stopped her from going to the kitchen, because it was dangerous for her. She was the one who cooked meals and took care of the room, because the children would go to school and I was busy with my own studies. Because she was now unable to do very much at all, it was becoming difficult. We were facing problems.

Nasreen started to see a doctor and that doctor checked her condition and said it was not very good. The doctor wanted to admit her to hospital and said that she would be taken good care of there. Nasreen didn't agree to that, but she kept on going to the doctor and to the nurse for counselling. The nurse was such a great person. He talked with her about Pakistani culture and many discussions took place. After visiting the doctor and getting proper counselling, Nasreen felt better. She was again talking to her children and was happy with them.

We were not the only victims of stress and trauma; there were many other people besides us who were not in the best phases of their lives. Some of these stressed people used to harm themselves and also violated the rules. During this period, we realised that refugees have very stressful and depressive lives. There were, and still are, thousands of refugees who go through different traumas and need support, guidance and proper counselling. Some people contemplated suicide when they were refused asylum, and also when they went through the long period of waiting, having to follow the long asylum procedure, while not being allowed to work, and living a destitute life.

Chapter Seventeen
Help and Support

Our journey was not easy; our social life, especially, was very disturbed at the beginning. We had no contact with people, because nearly everyone in the camp spoke Arabic and we couldn't. So, we stayed mostly in our rooms in isolation. Even if we went for a walk, we were mostly alone because we had no friends; it felt very bad. We could only talk to each other, but that was not enough; we needed some friends. There was also no one from our country to start with, and we felt lonely at that time.

As mentioned earlier, as time passed, we found our way to the church because initially, we knew nothing about Katwijk. But, later, we knew our way around. In the church, we were new and we needed to make contact, but people didn't seem interested at first. But we did get to know people, as explained earlier. One of those people was Erna Geurts, a wonderful lady.

Erna Geurts was like an angel sent from heaven for us. She became one of our best friends in the Netherlands. She thought a lot about us and did some great things to help us. She invited us to her house many times. We were always welcomed in her house and she was always welcomed by us.

Erna gave us Dutch lessons. One of the first words we learned was *rammelaar* (toy). It was difficult for us to learn, but we did! We also taught Erna to say the same word in Urdu, but she couldn't pronounce it. Even now when we meet, we always talk about this.

Our room was not big enough to accommodate many people as well as our stuff, so it looked a bit messy. But she never said anything about it. Instead, she enjoyed coming to our place to have a cup of coffee and talk to us. She once arranged with us to go to the Anne Frank House, so that we could take a break from our daily tensions. We had loads of fun with her.

She loved Nimra the most and Nimra also loved her. She felt as if she had found a grandmother in Erna. Erna also bought Anne Frank's book for Nimra.[8] Not only that, she also let celebrate Nimra's eighteenth birthday at her house because she thought that a camp was not an ideal place for the celebration of an eighteenth birthday, with it being a very important age for a teenager. She had her own problems going on, but she still decided to celebrate the special day. She also took us to her son's house and her friend's house. We were, and still are, very happy to have a friend like Erna – she is not only our friend, but a part of our family.

---

[8] Anne Frank, *The Diary of a Young Girl* (London: Puffin, 2007). Our version was *Anne Frank: Het Achterhuis* (Amsterdam: Prometheus, 2015).

I made friends with Marten van der Meer and he was also very kind to us. Nasreen and Nimra love flowers and I shared that with him. One day, Marten took us to Lisse and showed us lots of beautiful tulips. We took many pictures and enjoyed it a lot.

Besides these people, we made friends with many others, who also came to our place for dinner. Pastor Michel Hagen, who was the parish priest, and assistant parish priest Boris Plavčić also came to our room. They even had dinner with us. We felt embarrassed because we couldn't do much for them. We had no proper place or utensils but they never showed us that they did not like this. They were happy to have dinner with us.

Father Boris said that we didn't have to be worried about all this because he knew how it felt, as he himself had lived in the camp. He made us feel less worried. We were very pleased to see that they were happy while having dinner with us. Father Boris also took Nimra and Aroon with his family to Keukenhof to help them escape from the camp's atmosphere. That was a good outing for both the children.

Not only the above-mentioned people but many others helped us. Mr Jan van de Plas was also a very good friend of ours. He invited us to his home for Christmas dinner. We cooked some of the dishes and some were prepared by him. He made a meal of prawns and salmon for us. We had never eaten prawns before that day and it felt a bit weird, but we ate them because we could feel his love in the food he had prepared. In Pakistan, seafood such as prawns and crab are available only in the coastal areas, so we had never had the chance to taste them. We felt welcomed in his house and we loved it. He also took us for a one-day trip to Zeeland to show the construction projects known as the Delta Works. These are a series of constructions that were built to protect part of Holland from the sea. After visiting these places, we had dinner together in a Chinese restaurant, which we liked very much.

When Nasreen went to the chapel doing volunteer work, she made many friends who were also very kind. Her friend's names were Melinda and Marci. These ladies were very generous and helped Nasreen to get more social contacts. Melinda also came to our room and had lunch with us.

We felt very good when people came to our room. Marci was a big-hearted person. She took Nasreen to meet different people, to make more friends. Marci also introduced the whole family to some other friends of hers, Sofi and Paul. They were also very kind. In a short time, we all became good friends. Paul and Sofi's family and Marci's husband also came for dinner in our room. We had a lot of fun meeting them and having them for dinner. But they also invited us to their homes to eat and to spend time with them there.

There was also a young lady named Inge, mentioned earlier, who was leading the girls' group in the chapel as a volunteer, to help girls relax and forget about the refugee camp environment. She was very kind and generous. We knew her through Nimra, because Nimra used to go to that girls' club and liked it very much. Inge gave me very basic lessons in Dutch at the start, to help me learn! Then she became a good friend of us all. We got to meet her mother and the rest of the family, and we were also invited to their house a couple of times. They were very kind, showing us their city, Delft, and the important places there.

During our stay in the camp, a journalist came to interview us for the diocesan magazine *Tussenbeide*. She was a very open-hearted lady. She interviewed us and then also became a good friend. On Easter day, she invited us to her home for lunch and her family was very welcoming. We went to church with them. Later, we all went to see the Europoort in Rotterdam, which was a nice day. After coming back, we had lunch and played a game where we had to find Easter eggs. It was lots of fun.

We had heard that Dutch people don't invite too many people to their homes and do not like to talk for long… But with us it was a whole different story! We were welcomed into the homes of many Dutch people. They all opened their front doors and hearts to us. We found that they are very social, communicative, cordial and lovely people.

Through our experiences, we saw that contacts are very important in human life. Through the contacts we made, we were able to escape a lot of frustration. Normally, in a camp, people get food and accommodation and other very basic needs. But life is not just about food and accommodation. Human beings are not like animals, who just need food and sleep. The refugees need contacts, possibilities, opportunities and activities. All these contacts, help and support, and voluntary activities can lessen the burden of frustration and relieve stress.

Chapter Eighteen
The Fruit of Patience

By the start of December 2014, we had finished our official interviews with the IND. With the help of these interviews, the IND was supposed to decide whether we would be allowed to stay in the Netherlands or not. Then our lawyer had informed us that the IND needed more time to make a decision about our stay in this country. After we had been shifted to Pagedal, we were moved to Katwijk, where we were supposed to wait for the final decision.

On one Sunday morning in mid-February 2015, as we were getting ready to go to church, I went to check the post at the main reception in Katwijk. Our lawyer had sent us a letter. We tried to translate that letter from Dutch to English but at that time none of us could speak or understand Dutch, although we tried to get an idea through Google Translate! We worked out through Google's translation that the IND had given a pre-decision that was not positive. That was a tense day for us. We didn't know what would happen next or what our future would be.

On the Monday morning we went to the VluchtelingenWerk Nederland (VWN)[9] office for further information and proceedings. One of the workers from VWN read the letter and told us that the IND had not yet given us a negative decision, but that it was planning to do so. She also told us that we still had one chance to convince them by providing them more proof to counter their likely negative decision. We also called our lawyer, to ask, 'What kind of proof does the IND need from us?' and she guided us very well.

Somehow, within one month, we managed to gather all the proof and delivered this to the IND with the help of our lawyer. Our lawyer informed us that we needed to wait for another six months, until the IND had made a new final decision. It was quite a difficult time waiting for that decision. It was stressful for us, not knowing what was going to happen, but we were obliged to wait. When these six months were about to end, we were eagerly waiting to hear what the IND had decided. We again received a letter from our lawyer, but this time Nimra and Aroon were able to read it themselves. The letter stated that the IND was not still convinced with the new proof and, once again, was not intending to give a positive decision.

After our second pre-decision we were very disheartened because the IND was once again dissatisfied with our new proof. We felt that nobody wanted us and we were all alone in this world. Our lawyer, on the other hand,

---

[9] Dutch Council for Refugees.

said that together we were going to make the IND change their pre-decisions. This gave us hope and we felt encouraged. After that, our lawyer asked us to provide some more proof to show to the IND. Later on, she sent new documents to them. Our case was again put on hold and we had to wait nearly another six months.

In January 2016, we received the final decision from the IND, which was also negative. We were broken inside and felt as if we were losing the only little bit of hope we had left. It was a very sad moment for us. However, our lawyer was still optimistic regarding our case. She kept telling us that there was still hope about winning the case, through court. We had no other option except to go to court and we told our lawyer that we would definitely like to. We would not give up!

After three weeks, we got a date for our hearing in a court in Groningen. Our lawyer presented our case to the judge. This was the first time we had been to court in our lives. We had no idea how things worked in a court. We always thought that it would be a very scary scene, but it was not like we had originally imagined. The judge, his secretary and both lawyers seemed to be very kind and professional.

The judge was in no doubt regarding our case and thought that the IND should change their decision. The judge was convinced that the IND had not made their decision correctly! He gave the IND three months to do further research and reach a new decision.

After our hearing, we had a short discussion with our lawyer, and she was quite satisfied with the judge's positive approach towards our case. She told us that there was great hope that we could get a positive decision from the IND this time.

When three months had passed, we received another letter, saying that the IND needed more time to come to a new decision. This wait seemed to never end. After some time, we were told through our lawyer that the IND had decided to retract their earlier decision and would make a new decision shortly. It could be positive or negative, but we had to wait once again.

On 2nd June 2016, I was going to Amsterdam by train. On the way, at Haarlem railway station, I received a phone call from the lawyer's office. I now had a mobile, but I did not hear the phone ringing because of the noise of the train! Later, when I noticed that I had missed a call from the lawyer, I got scared.

At that very moment, thousands of thoughts crossed my mind. I called the lawyer's office and the secretary immediately said, 'Mr Javed, there is great news for you and your family. The IND has decided to give you and your family a permit to stay in the Netherlands!' I couldn't believe my ears and asked if what I'd heard was true. I got very excited and thanked her for this message.

After absorbing this and believing that it was the truth, I called Nasreen, who was in the camp. After hearing that, she was filled with joy and there were tears in her eyes. She thanked God for listening to their prayers and answering them.

The children were at school. I called Nimra and Aroon. When Nimra heard the news, she broke down in tears and couldn't hide her happiness. She went to her friends and, while still crying, told them that the family could stay in the Netherlands. The teacher came and congratulated her, then told the rest of the teachers and everyone came and congratulated both Aroon and Nimra.

Later in the day, when the family came together, we celebrated and gave thanks to God for helping us and listening to our prayers. The next Sunday, at our request, Father Boris offered a special Mass in thanksgiving for God's grace in helping us through a particularly challenging and difficult time.

Everyone now had new hopes and dreams for the future. This happiness made us forget all the hardships that we had faced in the past two years. Patience may at times be bitter, but its fruit is sweet.

Chapter Nineteen
Surprising Visits

Living in the camp, we had many hard moments but also some joyful and exciting times, which we still remember and will remember forever.

During our stay in Katwijk, we used to do volunteer work with IWAK, as well as receive lessons in the Dutch language and in cultural integration. One day we were informed by the IWAK volunteers that their organisation was conducting a meeting with one of the ministers from the parliament of the Netherlands.

The main goal of this meeting was to update the minister on the activities they were doing for the refugees of Katwijk. All the volunteers were assigned specific responsibilities, and they had to tell the minister about their activities and the work they were doing for refugees.

We prepared for this meeting with a lot of excitement and passion, without knowing exactly who the minister would be. This meeting was to be held on 6th July 2016 and we were asked by IWAK to be there at least half an hour before the beginning of the meeting. We arrived at the meeting location on schedule. We noticed that there were special arrangements, and we observed that it was the first time that an IWAK gathering was very official and formal. Anybody who entered the meeting place went through a security checkpoint.

When we entered the hall, we realised that everyone was formally dressed. The meeting hall was properly arranged and decorated, and every group had a presentation and was seated accordingly.

Before the start of the meeting, the chair of IWAK spoke to us about the programme and told us not to use our mobile phones or any means of communication. He also told us that there was a huge surprise for us and everyone was wondering what the surprise would be.

Eventually he told us that there would be no minister coming, but that the King of the Netherlands, Willem-Alexander himself, was coming to visit us. It was a huge surprise. We looked at each other with open mouths and started clapping. He told us that they had not been allowed to disclose this earlier for security reasons. After this huge announcement, everyone kept their eyes on the main entrance and wondered when the king would arrive.

At last the wait ended and the king arrived. The feeling we had when we saw him can't be put into words. It was a moment that we will cherish for the whole of our lives. Our eyes just couldn't believe that the king was with us.

He visited every group and our group was the one he visited first. He came and sat right next to us, and tried his best to talk individually to everyone. We personally told him how our life in the camp was going, and about our daily life. We also explained how IWAK and the churches of Katwijk were playing an important role in the lives of refugees, and how they were trying to help refugees in this bad phase of their lives. He asked us about the situation of Christian people in our native country and what jobs we had been doing in our homeland. I told him that we were planning to write a book about our experiences and our stay in the camp.

After talking with our cultural and educational group, he went on to talk with other groups, such as the Bible study group, sports group, youth group, clothing group and prayer group.

We found him very kind and friendly. He went away after spending an hour with us, but he never went away from our hearts and memories. When we arrived back in the camp, we told our children about this event and they went crazy: 'If you had told us about the king, we would have come there!' they said.

The very next week, a teacher from the language school run for refugees by the COA came and told us that today there was a special lesson arranged for us and we should come and attend it. We got an idea from the COA that someone special was coming.

When we went for the lesson, we found out that the Prime Minister, Mark Rutte, was coming that day to pay a visit to the refugees and to see the life they were living. Our excitement went to another level! It was another precious moment of our lives when we met the Prime Minister of the Netherlands. He came to our Dutch language lesson and sat with us. He also taught us a few Dutch words himself.

After visiting our class, he walked through whole of the camp and tried to have a little chat with people. We were able to introduce our children to the Prime Minister. Everyone was happy to see him and was running towards him, wanting to have a photo taken with him.

After meeting these two big personalities of the Netherlands, we realised that both of them were very polite and met us very generously. We were quite inspired by their attitude of kindness and openness. It was a visible sign of solidarity and harmony from their side with the refugees.

Later in this same month of July, we also got the chance to go to a Catholic church in Brielle and had the privilege of meeting Mgr Dr J H J van den Hende, Bishop of Rotterdam diocese. We met him personally and told him about ourselves. It was, and will always remain, one of the most memorable months in our lives in the camp, as we met three very inspiring people.

When we told our parish priest, Father Michel Hagen, that we had met 'the king, the prime minister and the bishop', he was very surprised and said in a playful way that now only the Pope was left. After the Mass ended, he made an announcement to the church about our meetings with these important people.

Everyone in the church was amazed to hear that. Many people came to greet and congratulate us afterwards, even those people who never usually talked to us! They were asking us all kinds of different questions about these meetings. They all said that we were very lucky to have seen the king, the prime minister and the bishop in such a short period. Later, this news was published in the church magazine, *De Augustinus*, with our photos. So, in this way, we came to know more people in the church and more people came to know us.

Chapter Twenty
Open Day

During our stay in Katwijk, the COA twice organised an 'Open Dag' (Open Day). On that day, everyone could visit the camp and have a tour. It was a day on which people got a chance to interact with the different cultures and to find out about the refugees. On a normal, regular day, not many people could visit because they needed to inform reception before entering the camp and the rooms.

On the Open Day, refugees from different cultures and beliefs were able to show the visitors various aspects of their cultures, customs, food and traditions. They prepared numerous stalls with food from different countries. People organised fashion shows to exhibit their cultural attire. Music from different countries was played and people danced and had fun. Besides that, people could get information about the procedures that the refugees underwent in order to get their residence permits.

The COA staff asked us to have a stall with Pakistani food. At that time, we were about to leave the camp, and were busy decorating our new home, so it was difficult for us to say yes immediately. Still, we agreed to participate in the Open Day, to show our respect for them. Because of the Open Day, the kitchen was open the whole night so that the people participating could prepare the food. We had done most of the preparations before sleeping, and the next morning woke up early to prepare the rest.

While cooking the food we had to keep a lot of things in mind, like adding less spice than usual. Pakistani food is mostly spicy, so we had to adjust the spices according to Dutch food tastes! We enjoyed ourselves while carrying out all these preparations. When we had finished cooking, we went to the hall to decorate our stall with some Pakistani items. We hung examples of our cultural dress, some bangles, some beautifully decorated Pakistani hand fans, some pictures, and the map and flag of Pakistan.

There were stalls from different countries, such as Afghanistan, Eritrea, China, Kenya, Iran, Iraq, Somalia and Syria. Everyone decorated their stalls beautifully, and all the stalls represented the culture of those countries. The refugees dressed in their national clothing. There were food stalls, dance performances and different fun shows.

For children, the COA organised a stall where some girls did face painting for them and put henna on their hands. Besides that, there was a variety of swings for children. There were some information desks about the COA, IND, VWN, GGD[10] and many other organisations helping the refugees.

---

[10] Public Health Service.

People were enjoying themselves. All the refugees and visitors were going to the stalls, trying different foods, getting information, talking to people and playing with children. Almost all the stalls were very busy, with many people gathered around them – except one: the IND information desk. Refugees were a bit scared to go there because many of them were still going through the asylum procedure or had just completed it. We went there and made a kind of joke to the IND workers, saying: 'All the stalls are fully occupied but yours is not very busy. We think that people fear you!' They laughed.

On the information desk, we saw a book: *Ik Ben Miran* (*My Name is Miran*).[11] It is a collection of stories of refugee children and their experiences of refugee life. We found this book very interesting and wanted to buy it, but they had only one copy with them. So, later, we bought it from a book store. We met many people, talked to them and made friends. We also visited various food stalls, drank coffee/tea/juices, danced and tried many different things.

Eventually, it was the time for the sun to set. We had to pack all our things away and head back to our rooms. But it was a time that we could never forget. We saw smiles on the faces of people who were usually depressed and had no hope. Every person we knew was filled with joy. They all forgot about their worries and problems for a while.

Days like this play a very important role in the lives of refugees. These joyful moments last for a lifetime and take a special place in our hearts. That day was very memorable, and we were glad to have participated in the

---

[11] Anne-Marieke Samson, *Ik Ben Miran* (Amsterdam: Ploegsma, 2016).

event. The Open Day brought together the refugees, different organisations, churches and the Dutch community. Plus, it celebrated cultural diversity. This day left a message that we should not think only about ourselves, but also about those people who are around us. We should celebrate the diversity of our human community and we should work together for the betterment of humanity.

Chapter Twenty-one
The Lord Builds the House

After we had obtained the residence permit, the COA started the process of finding a house for us. We requested, if it were possible, a house in Leiden, as our children were studying there. We didn't want our children to shift schools, because if they went to one in another place they would have to repeat the whole school year.

The COA told us that only if the school issued a letter stating that it was essential for the children to stay in the area surrounding Leiden would there be a possibility of getting a house there. Otherwise, we could get a place anywhere in the country. The school administration gave us the letter, which we gave to the COA. After one week we found out that our request had been accepted and we had been allotted the city of Leiden.

We were excited and eagerly waiting to go to our own house. During this time, we were informed by the COA that we might get a flat, as most of the people in Leiden live in flats. I was a bit nervous when I heard this, as I have a phobia about heights. However, at the beginning of September 2016, we discovered that the new home allotted to us was a house! We were very happy because, after more than two years, we were to begin a new phase of our lives. At the same time, we were astonished by the way God's providence was coming in abundance.

We were waiting impatiently to get into our house; but, on the other hand, we were trying to figure out how to arrange and do all the decorating work needed. At last, on 21st September 2016, with the help of VWN Leiden, we officially visited our house, signed the contract with the housing company, and got the keys. It was a moment of joy. We finally felt that our lives were going to restart and be 'normal' again.

There was a lot of work needed at our new home – painting, flooring, furnishings, garden etc. We told all of our friends about the house and also told them that there was a lot of work to be done. We received messages and emails saying that everyone was ready to help us in every possible way!

The next day, a friend of ours came from Delft and went with Nasreen to do all the necessary shopping. They bought all the things that were needed to get the house in order. Nasreen, that lady and I immediately started painting the walls. We also gave the house keys to some of our friends and whenever they had time they went in and did some work. Our friends' contributions were important in settling us into our house. All of them gave us their time and energy in many different ways.

We completed our kitchen very rapidly because it was difficult for us to carry food every day from Katwijk. We also slept a few nights on the kitchen floor, so we could invest more time in the renovation work. Although it was difficult to sleep on the floor, we had the feeling of homeliness.

One Sunday we went to the church, as it was our last Holy Mass in H Joannes de Doper, Katwijk, and when we came back it was raining. We saw that one of our friends, Sofi, was busy in the garden, despite the rain, while Paul was working on the curtains in the house. We fully felt their real involvement and support.

After working day and night, and with the help of our friends, within three weeks our house was finally ready to live in. Two of our friends from Katwijk helped us to move our stuff from Katwijk to Leiden. In the same way, some of our friends helped us to get furniture and some other things from different places to our house.

When our house was finished, it looked really beautiful, and everyone was happy. We invited Father Boris to bless our house and, later on, three other Catholic priests – Michel Hagen, Piet Koomen and Sjaak de Boer – and many other friends came to visit us.

After living for almost a year in Leiden, one morning I received a call from one of my friends, Mark, who, along with me and other volunteer teachers, gave catechism classes on Sundays in the pastoral centre of the Roman Catholic Church of Our Saviour in Den Haag. Mark told me that he wanted to give his car to us, as a gift! I told the family about the unexpected gift and we thanked the Lord. Although we had received other provision, this time it was like a big miracle!

As I write, we have begun a new phase in our family life. Nimra and Aroon are in the last years of their high school studies, Nasreen and I are doing Dutch language courses at Leiden University and, besides this, I am studying for a Master's in Peace, Trauma and Religion at Vrije Universiteit, Amsterdam. Although we have started a normal life in this new house, we remember the words: 'Unless the LORD builds the house, the builders labour in vain' (Psalm 127:1).

Chapter Twenty-two
The Ways of Integration

There are many problems faced by refugees when they migrate from their own country to another one. In the Netherlands, there are also some issues that refugees have to face while integrating into Dutch society. According to our experience, some of these problems include language barriers, housing, food, transportation, educational issues, medication, the weather, laws and regulations, employment issues, isolation, skills and qualifications, the stress of adaptation, clashing and negotiation of two cultures, cultural identity, economic difficulties and missing the native country, to name just a few!

We are registered with Gemeente Leiden (Municipality of Leiden). This helps status holders to integrate with Dutch society through various projects. We participated in an integration course from December 2016 to May 2017. The main goal of this course was adaptation to Dutch culture and society. In our opinion, the course was very informative and helpful in the process of adapting to our new culture.

During this course we learned that in the Netherlands everyone has the same rights and everyone must abide by the same rules. Everyone has a freedom to express their opinions, freedom to have faith or not, and to be open about their sexuality. All citizens are treated equally, and there is no discrimination according to gender or belief. All citizens are responsible for society.

The mentor project is also part of integration on an individual basis. Each status holder gets a Dutch mentor with whom the status holder remains in personal contact. Marianne was appointed as my mentor, and Maria was appointed as mentor to Nasreen. We met with our mentors weekly and tried to speak Dutch with them. Dutch is a difficult language, which takes time to learn. But our mentors encouraged us to speak with them in Dutch.

We talked with our mentors about different topics, such as cultural differences, traditions and values. In spite of all the differences, they tried to give us a sense of being 'at home' in this country, giving us exposure to different places in the city and surroundings. The main purpose of these visits was to gain knowledge and to understand the history of the society in which we were now living. In this regard, Marianne organised a trip to visit Volendam, which is well known for its old fishing boats and traditional clothing. We had pictures taken of us wearing traditional Dutch costumes.

We admire the fact that Gemeente Leiden is working hard towards the fast integration of the refugees, but adapting to a new society is a slow process. Cultural differences play a big role in the integration journey. Most refugees that come to the Netherlands have different cultural values. These differ in many ways from Western culture, for example in terms of dress, food, cultural norms, women's empowerment and gender biases.

Openness is a big factor to which refugees have to adjust. Dutch culture is direct and open about everything. In the Netherlands, refugees have to get used to this openness. Dutch culture is aimed towards individuality, and young people are independent from an early age. Refugees are mostly not independent, therefore they have a hard time while integrating.

Likewise, language can be a big problem. Language issues can mean a limited network. Learning our new country's language remains a challenge for us, but can lead us in the overall integration process.

There are many positive efforts to help people progress in the area of integration, but to create a sense of 'home' in refugees is an essential part of integration. Only by creating the sense of belonging can one truly feel at home.

Chapter Twenty-three
Destination Found?

In 2014 we left our home country and journeyed towards an unknown destination. Now, after a few years, we ask ourselves: 'Did we find a new destination?'

Of course, one can ask where an unknown destination ends. Did we reach it when we were granted resident status? Or when we started to live in our new house? There are still so many uncertainties in our lives. We are still learning Dutch, integrating into a new society and searching for possibilities of work, and life is not quite settled. Who knows what our 'final destination' will be in this country?

When we look back over the past few years, there is one thing we can say very firmly. An unknown destination is a place of uncertainties and instability. There is no guarantee or certainty of the future, and in finding ourselves in this place, we can easily become pessimistic. We can ask ourselves whether anything good can come out of an unknown destination.

So many times, we lost hope. Sometimes we didn't even want to go on. However, in this journey God taught us to trust Him. In such poor circumstances, He showed us His love and grace. We found His provision. For us, an unknown destination is, therefore, a place of mystery and dependence on God. It is place of going deeper into our spiritual lives, and relying on God.

It is an invitation to look beyond our present situation and difficulties, beyond our current circumstances, beyond the ordinary things of day-to-day life, and to look at new possibilities. It is an opportunity to shift our focus from the suffering that holds us back, and to go ahead with trust and patience, looking at the grace and love of God in this unknown destination. He is the only source of our faith and hope.

You may have had some experiences in your life like we did and found yourself spiralling downwards. We 'carried our cross'[12] and we embraced it in each situation. But later on, we discovered it is a way of life. As human beings we are limited, but God does many wonders with our limitations, and the experience of His wonders cannot let us down.

Let's look to the life of Abraham, in the Old Testament. In Genesis 12 we read that Abraham (then called Abram) also travelled towards an unknown destination (see verse 1). Maybe he didn't want to leave his own people, but he went because he trusted in God. The experience of Abraham can happen in our lives too. In fact, nobody

---

[12] See Luke 9:23.

knows what the future holds or where they will end up. But God knows.

We believe that there comes a time when God requires some sort of change in our way of living. That's why this experience can happen to all of us. He asks us to go in new directions. However, He does not provide us with Google Maps! It is a way of going ahead by faith. He is faithful and trustworthy, and nothing is impossible for God.

God takes our hands and leads us out from our difficulties and from our small ways of thinking. He lifts our hearts and minds to see beyond the situation and the circumstances that disappoint us. He takes us outside our limitations, and He prepares us for the new. God wants us to leave behind the old things, so we are able to embrace Him and the blessings of the new.

One of the keys to receiving His blessing is to do His will, to live in obedience ... and to leave the old ways of thinking so we can embrace the new. The new is always uncertain. There is no guarantee. It is painful, but what God did in the life of Abraham, He wants to do in our lives – sometimes that means moving on physically but, more importantly, it means changing the way we think and act as 'new creations' in Christ.[13] However, His ways of working do not always look like we think they should!

God wants us to start relying on Him. It is not easy moving from your country and going to an unknown destination. It is very difficult and uncomfortable. When you move, you do not know what will happen. But when we leave ourselves in His hands then He always amazes us

---

[13] See 2 Corinthians 5:17.

with His goodness. We remember the words of Jesus: 'Do not let your hearts be troubled. You believe in God; believe also in me' (John 14:1).

For us, we experienced the presence of God in this unknown destination. We found that God is interested in our circumstances. He showed His love, concern and care for us and was in our journey. His grace was greater than our limitations and fears. He led us and will continue to lead us as long as we follow Him. In this way, we will arrive eventually at our spiritual and divine destination.

Response to Javed's Story

by Dave Smith, founder and trustee of the Boaz Trust, which works to support asylum seekers in the UK. He is also the author of *The Book of Boaz* and *Refugee Stories*

How should we respond to Javed's story? In many ways, the Dutch asylum system is very different from the system in the UK. In the UK there are no large camps where asylum seekers are held while their claims are decided. Instead they live in smaller shared houses. The system for deciding an asylum case is also different, with an initial interview that leads to a decision to either accept or refuse the asylum claim, then the opportunity to appeal a negative decision and go to tribunal. Following this, a final decision is made, after which those refused are expected to leave the country.

Yet however different the two systems may be, the experience of the asylum seeker is remarkably similar. Being uprooted from home and all that is familiar, being in an alien culture and struggling to understand a strange language are all difficult to cope with, especially if you are already suffering from trauma as a result of persecution in your own country. The alienation felt by the one seeking sanctuary is compounded by a system that appears not to want you, and by officials who are often suspicious and uncaring. It is little wonder that almost every sanctuary seeker experiences stress, anxiety and depression, just as Javed and Nasreen did, even though they had a strong faith. In the UK, the sad truth is that it is the norm for those seeking sanctuary to be on antidepressants.

I believe there are a number of major factors that contribute to this depression, all of which could be relatively easily addressed.

Firstly, asylum seekers have nothing to do except sit and watch TV. They are not allowed to work, which, for men especially, destroys their sense of dignity and self-worth. For women, not being able to create a home has a similar effect. I have seen people with real talents, such as doctors and engineers, become demotivated, deskilled and dehumanised. By the time they eventually get their refugee status, they have lost all self-confidence and struggle to find employment. In the UK there have been huge cuts to ESOL (English) classes, meaning that it's really difficult to learn the language; you can't even fill your empty time with study.

Secondly, the interminable waiting for no apparent reason plays on the mind in a destructive way. 'Why haven't I heard yet? Surely the evidence I gave must be enough? Does this waiting mean they don't believe me? What is taking so long? Have they lost my papers?' Again, cuts in the numbers of asylum caseworkers have meant that decisions are now taking longer. It is not uncommon for even the initial decision to take well over six months, and for a case to still be unresolved several years after arrival in the UK.

Thirdly, there is the feeling of not being wanted. This is not surprising when one of the first things you are told on claiming asylum in the UK is that there is a Voluntary Returns programme. As the process to decide your case goes on, there is nothing that dispels that unwanted feeling. Even the opportunity to have a face-to-face appointment with an official no longer exists. Now you can only ring the Migrant Help number for information and advice.

Javed and Nasreen came through their ordeal because they patiently waited for God. They came through because they decided to make the very best of their situation by serving others, volunteering and doing far more than their share of cleaning and other duties. They put Colossians 3:23 into practice by doing everything as if they were doing it for the Lord. They also came through because they had friends who supported them, whether it was by inviting them for a meal, showing them around the town or finding bikes for them so they could get around!

So, what can we do to make life for those seeking sanctuary in our country more bearable? I guess it depends where you live: if you don't live in an asylum dispersal area, then you may not be able to directly meet those seeking asylum, but there are things that you can do:

- You can pray for those seeking sanctuary, for the caseworkers and immigration judges who have to decide their futures, and for our government that makes the policies that influence those decisions. Pray that the 'hostile environment' becomes a 'hospitable environment' where the stranger is welcomed.

- You can give to charities that are supporting refugees and asylum seekers. Many rely heavily on donations, as there is very little statutory funding for what they do, and charitable grants are not easy to access.

- You can campaign for changes in the asylum system. Simple changes like granting those in the system the right to work after six months would make a huge difference to the well-being of asylum seekers.

- You can find out if there are any Syrian Resettlement houses nearby. Some councils have signed up to take Syrian families, through the government scheme. Churches and community groups have also raised funds to provide homes for Syrians through the Community Sponsorship scheme. If you don't have a scheme in your area, why not consider starting one yourself?

If you do live in a dispersal area – which applies mainly to all the larger towns and cities in the UK – especially in the areas where housing is cheaper, then you can get directly involved. There may be asylum seekers or refugees in your church, but even if there aren't, there will be local drop-ins or support agencies where you can get involved. So these are the three key things you can do:

- Find out where the asylum seekers are, and how you can meet them. Once you have met them, you will begin to see how you can help.

- Be a friend. More than anything else, people need friends, and asylum seekers more than anyone. Having someone who will listen, empathise and share their life is more important than anything else.

- Walk with them through their troubles. It makes a huge difference to have someone who can explain how things work in the UK, who will take time to show them round, who will go with them to their tribunal hearing or help them move into their accommodation when they are eventually granted their refugee status.

As you do these things you will help others, like Javed and Nasreen, to integrate well and become people who contribute to and change their adopted country for the better.

UK Sources of Information and Help

If you want to be more involved in helping UK asylum seekers and refugees, then there are places where you can find what you are looking for.

The Refugee Resource Centre for Churches, or R2C2 for short, has a wealth of information on everything from how the asylum system works to a map pinpointing hundreds of local projects. The How You Can Help section is particularly useful. The website address is:
www.refugeeresourcecentreforchurches.org.uk

Welcome Churches is a charity that offers training to local churches in welcoming asylum seekers and refugees. It has years of expertise from working in a multicultural church in Derby where many who came to seek sanctuary in the UK have found Jesus Christ as their ultimate sanctuary. They also initiated Welcome Boxes as a means of welcoming new arrivals into their city. You can find them at:
www.welcomechurches.org